ASHE Higher Education Report: Volume 40, Number 6
Kelly Ward, Lisa E. Wolf-Wendel, Series Editors

Student Engagement Online: What Works and Why

Katrina A. Meyer

Student Engagement Online: What Works and Why
Katrina A. Meyer
ASHE Higher Education Report: Volume 40, Number 6
Kelly Ward, Lisa E. Wolf-Wendel, Series Editors

Cover image by © Anastasia Ku/iStockphoto

ISSN 1551-6970   electronic ISSN 1554-6306   ISBN 978-1-119-00075-4

The ASHE Higher Education Report is part of the Jossey-Bass Higher and Adult Education Series and is published six times a year by Wiley Subscription Services, Inc., A Wiley Company, at Jossey-Bass, One Montgomery Street, Suite 1200, San Francisco, California 94104-4594.

Individual subscription rate (in USD): $174 per year US/Can/Mex, $210 rest of world; institutional subscription rate: $352 US, $412 Can/Mex, $463 rest of world. Single copy rate: $29. Electronic only–all regions: $174 individual, $352 institutional; Print & Electronic–US: $192 individual, $423 institutional; Print & Electronic–Canada/Mexico: $192 individual, $483 institutional; Print & Electronic–Rest of World: $228 individual, $534 institutional. See the Back Issue/Subscription Order Form in the back of this volume.

CALL FOR PROPOSALS: Prospective authors are strongly encouraged to contact Kelly Ward (kaward@wsu.edu) or Lisa E. Wolf-Wendel (lwolf@ku.edu). See "About the ASHE Higher Education Report Series" in the back of this volume.

Visit the Jossey-Bass Web site at **www.josseybass.com.**

Printed in the United States of America on acid-free recycled paper.

The ASHE Higher Education Report is indexed in CIJE: Current Index to Journals in Education (ERIC), Education Index/Abstracts (H.W. Wilson), ERIC Database (Education Resources Information Center), Higher Education Abstracts (Claremont Graduate University), IBR & IBZ: International Bibliographies of Periodical Literature (K.G. Saur), and Resources in Education (ERIC).

Advisory Board

The ASHE Higher Education Report Series is sponsored by the Association for the Study of Higher Education (ASHE), which provides an editorial advisory board of ASHE members.

Contents

Executive Summary

Why Engagement?

With more students needing a higher education and less resources available from the states, the productivity of higher education institutions has become of greater interest to state governments, national foundations, and other assorted groups. Given its importance to individuals and the economy, President Obama has stressed the need for higher education to control its costs and produce more and better graduates. By moving academic programs and coursework online, higher education institutions must ensure that students succeed in their online programs.

Given the highly visible research on the National Study of Student Engagement (NSSE) and what it has revealed about engagement in the face-to-face environment, it makes sense to investigate the ways that engagement strategies can keep students enrolled in their online programs to completion and ensure they are learning what they need to succeed. This monograph presents the research on student engagement online and draws recommendations for instructors designing or teaching an online course.

Are There Limits to Engagement?

Students' lives tend to present serious limits to what can be achieved with engagement strategies. They have employment or family demands that force them to attend part-time or they may be inexperienced students and need to "learn how to learn" or to understand the basics of online learning. They may need to develop self-regulatory behaviors, motivation to succeed, and the ability to defer gratification. They may also have to develop an understanding of and skills for active learning and find time and willingness to put effort into their learning.

Instructors also sometimes act in ways that impinge on student engagement, by offering poorly designed online courses, dominating course interactions, and being unclear about the educational goals of course activities and what students are expected to achieve. These instructors may need to improve their online teaching skills or their understanding of how students learn; this may involve examining their expectations of what "instruction" is and what it is that instructors do to bring learning about.

What Works to Increase Student Engagement in Online Coursework?

The main goal of the monograph is to identify the approaches or techniques that have been proven to increase engagement. To achieve this goal, the monograph draws upon learning theories and research studies conducted in online learning courses and also some face-to-face situations.

Use Learning Theories That Encourage Engagement

Put simply, engagement strategies work because they are based on learning theories that stress student activity rather than passive learning. Active learning, collaborative learning, authentic and experiential learning, as well as several other theories that focus on getting the student to do something—be it cognitive or physical—work to engage them in their learning. These learning theories are "why" engagement works.

Focus on Pedagogies and Active Learning Options

Pedagogies that stress student effort or work tend to engage more effectively. That means using assignments that ask students to do something—such as work in a group, solve a problem, prepare a project, and experience a situation—will more likely produce student engagement in his or her learning.

Interact for an Educational Purpose
Be it for online discussions, group work, or simple email exchanges, students need to know the goal and reason for the assignment. Instructors need to provide not only the goal, but also the rationale for the assignment, explaining what it will help students learn and why it is being done in this way.

Push Students to Think More Deeply
Whether in the design of assignments, directions to students about the assignments, or the evaluation criteria for students' work, instructors need to ask questions, critique student responses, and provide additional context for the learning. Instructors also need to show students what deep thinking is.

Teach Students How to Learn
Not all students arrive at college with the skills to learn. College-level instructors are increasingly called upon to not only teach students how to learn online, but also to help them develop self-discipline and other self-regulatory behaviors.

Evaluate Tools, Both Hardware and Software
Developers will continue to work on improving existing online tools and creating new ones. Instructors will need to evaluate these tools in the online course to assess their impact on student engagement and learning and share their findings with others.

Evaluate Online Classes Over and Over Again
Instructors need to undertake more detailed evaluations of what happens in their online classes and focus on individual elements to determine what works for engagement and student learning and what does not.

Assess Student Engagement and Its Effect on Retention and Learning
Too often, research on engagement strategies has used engagement as the final outcome measure. But research also needs to chronicle engagement's effect on

student retention and learning to provide comparisons among engagement strategies and to help make the case that engagement is worth the extra effort.

Are There Differences in Engagement Between Online and Face to Face?

The research so far indicates that engagement may be engagement in both settings. The learning theories, pedagogies, and activities used in the course produce student engagement whether the course is online or face-to-face.

Foreword

Online learning and student engagement are topics that are familiar in research and practice related to higher education. What has been missing, however, is a focus on how the two concepts are integrated and inform one another. The focus of Katrina A. Meyer's monograph, *Student Engagement Online: What Works and Why*, is the importance of student engagement in online education. The monograph provides valuable foundational information that is sure to be useful as more institutions grapple with how to best engage all students.

Institutions are compelled toward online learning as a means to tap broader audiences of students and to recruit beyond geographically bounded markets. Online learning for many campuses has meant an increase in diversity of students and a means to stay financially solvent. With the expansion, however, have come challenges associated with retention. An important component of retention in any setting is student engagement. Engagement is tied to positive student outcomes. Based, in part, on the evidence of the National Survey of Student Engagement, concepts related to student engagement in all aspects of the college experience are important to the student experience. In particular, current research suggests links between student engagement and student completion. The focus of student engagement has largely been on traditional campus environments. Meyer's work expands the importance of student engagement from a focus on campus venues to online settings.

The monograph fills an important void because most of the research about student engagement is based on traditional college students in brick and mortar settings, and much of the online learning literature is focused on nontraditional students and baseline outcomes, and tends toward descriptive and proscriptive approaches. The monograph synthesizes the points of overlap between online learning and student engagement and why it is important to pay attention to what needs to change in terms of learning and development in online settings. The findings of the emerging research suggest the importance of paying attention to student involvement and engagement in online settings. The monograph is sure to be of use to staff, faculty, and administrators associated with online learning as well as people who are engaging in research to more fully understand the totality of student engagement and online learning. The topics covered are helpful to provide basic and foundational information, including definitions and theory, as well as useful practical information about how to make online classes and programs more engaging. Faculty who teach in online settings will find the strategies and approaches Meyer presents particularly helpful. The analysis and synthesis of the literature is comprehensive and informative. Readers geared toward application will find useful and practical information, and readers geared toward research will find an expansive view on engagement and online education.

Failing to pay attention to student engagement in both online and on-campus environments means risking the loss of quality students who are perfectly capable of carrying out the academic work, but who find themselves disconnected from the learning environment. The ideas put forth in the monograph take some of the best practices and theories related to engagement and use them to inform the improvement of online learning and development. The monograph builds on previous topics in the ASHE Monograph Series related to online learning (e.g., *Cost Efficiencies in Online Learning*) and student success (e.g., *Piecing Together the Student Success Puzzle*) by providing updated information and making linkages between student engagement and online settings. Student success is important regardless of location of the learning experience, and Meyer's monograph provides information on how to make for a better learning experience for online students.

Kelly Ward
Lisa E. Wolf-Wendel
Series Editors

Published online in Wiley Online Library
(wileyonlinelibrary.com) • DOI: 10.1002/aehe.20018

Student Engagement in Online Learning: What Works and Why

Overview

WITH PRESSURES TO INCREASE ACCESS to higher education, colleges and universities have focused on increasing the number of online courses and programs offered. Higher education is also being criticized for its retention and graduation rates, and pressure is building to find solutions. To ensure that online learning can help address these problems, professionals dedicated to online learning are under pressure to explore and evaluate strategies for getting students engaged in their online studies. These pressures are the genesis and reason for this monograph.

By applying the theories and techniques for student engagement in online learning, instructors and designers of online courses can improve and increase student engagement and help higher education produce graduates who can contribute to their families, communities, and the economy. The theories and research reviewed in this monograph provide important clues as to how to help students learn, stay enrolled, and finish a degree.

Engagement techniques may be one key to making online learning productive for the institution but, more importantly, ensuring that students are successful as they pursue a college degree. In fact, achieving student engagement in online courses may be more important than it is in on-campus courses because online students have fewer ways to be engaged with the institution and perhaps greater demands on their time and attention as well. In other

---

words, engagement may be the critical key to making online learning an essential component of higher education and indispensable part of an institution's future.

By way of introduction to the monograph, this chapter presents more information on the various challenges to higher education at the current time and then provides a few essential definitions that inform the monograph. Then for those unfamiliar with the field of student engagement, the chapter presents a brief overview of the history of student engagement, as it has been developed to pertain to traditional instructional modes, with attention to the National Survey of Student Engagement (NSSE). The chapter discusses the major reasons for the interest in online learning and the subsequent importance of student engagement for online students. Finally, the chapter concludes with the relevance of the monograph to various professionals concerned with higher education and provides an overview of content in each subsequent chapter.

The Challenges

As higher education is increasingly urged to improve its ability to enroll more students, ensure student learning, and improve graduation rates, and to do all this more efficiently, higher education institutions are looking for solutions. Online learning has been adopted by many institutions as a way to expand access to instructional programs and address the increase in many states of recent high school graduates as well as adults seeking further education or training, and to do so with an eye to controlling costs or avoiding construction of new buildings. The cost issue, made worse during the most recent economic crisis, has meant declining state resources for public higher education, uncertain student enrollments as many students must delay college or enroll part time, and greater public attention to increasing tuition rates and student debt levels. Many institutions have adopted online learning as a way to address these problems. In Allen and Seaman's (2012) survey of higher education institutions, 86.5% of the 2,082 responding institutions offer online courses and 62.5% offer complete online degree programs.

Funding is an obviously critical issue that affects institutions and has led to a greater focus on online learning. Higher education institutions were deeply affected by budget cuts resulting from worsening economies in many states. Based on changes in state funding of public higher education from FY09 to FY10, 28 states appropriated monies that were 0.1 to 10.0% less, 10 more states appropriated monies that were 10.1 to 22.0% less, and 12 states appropriated the same or larger monies (Chronicle of Higher Education, 2011). These figures have improved by fiscal year 2012–2013, where 30 states increased their appropriations to higher education (Kelderman, 2013). Although these facts may imply an improvement in states' budgets and funding for higher education, the growing demands on states for K–12 improvement, healthcare reform, and other pressing concerns argue against such an interpretation. This more dim view of the future of higher education funding is supported by Moody's Investor Service (Kiley, 2013), which noted that all of the revenue streams that traditionally support higher education were undergoing pressure from economic, technological, and public opinion shifts. And these changes appear to be out of institutions' hands, forcing leaders to be more strategic and innovative in their efforts to improve institutional productivity, develop new markets and services, prioritize use of resources, and demonstrate value to those who fund higher education.

With more students and fewer resources, the productivity of higher education institutions has become of greater interest to state governments, national foundations, and other assorted groups. In a study of the effectiveness of states' performance-based funding programs, Tandberg and Hillman (2013) reviewed data on 25 states that have some version of performance-based funding for higher education institutions. These funding structures vary by the amount of the institution's budget subject to performance measures, the type of measures used, type of institution included, and the length of time the measures have been in operation. Despite findings that performance-based funding either affected outcomes after a long period of time (seven years) or had no effect at all (Tandberg & Hillman, 2013), several other states are exploring similar approaches to make funding of public higher education dependent on achieving state goals or productivity improvements. (One of these state goals has been increased access, which has fueled the interest in online learning.)

Several state performance-based funding systems stress the importance of addressing higher education institutions' less-than-sterling retention and graduation rates. The first-year retention rate (from fall 2008 to fall 2009) was 71.9% for full-time students (42.5% for part-time students) at all institutions (National Center for Education Statistics [NCES], 2011a). For two-year colleges, the first-year retention rate was 60.9% versus 77.8% at four-year institutions. The graduation rates for cohorts beginning in 2001 were 36.4% (for those completing within the traditional four-year timeframe) for all four-year institutions versus 17.9% for all two-year institutions (NCES, 2010). For those from the business sector, these rates represent inefficiencies or waste on the part of the institution as well as for students. These rates are different at various colleges because they may serve populations that arrive underprepared for college work or have other unique challenges. This means that the criticism leveled at colleges for poor retention and graduation rates is not solely the fault of the college, and yet it is reasonable to ask colleges to find ways to improve these rates by investigating better methods of educating students and ensuring they graduate. Colleges, staffed largely with able and dedicated persons, certainly have the capability to improve themselves.

The issue of retention is of particular interest in online education as well. However, data on retention of online programs are neither clear nor consistent. Jenkins (2011), citing "countless studies," claimed success rates in online courses "of only 50 percent—as opposed to 70-to-75 percent for comparable face-to-face classes" (Jenkins, 2011, para. 3). Unfortunately, such claims as this one are common in the popular literature and show neither online learning nor face-to-face courses in a particularly good light. A recent email exchange on a listserv about online retention rates elicited more detailed responses from representatives of several institutions (Meyer, 2012a). The California Community Colleges and Broward College had online retention rates that were 7% below face-to-face retention rates, and Montgomery College had a retention rate for online and blended courses that was 4% lower than for face-to-face courses. Both Athabasca University and the North Dakota University System found that 85% of undergraduate students finished their online courses. In a recent study of managers of online education (WICHE Cooperative for Educational Telecommunications [WCET], 2013), online course completion rates were 3% lower than on-campus course completion rates (78% versus 81%). On the other hand, the University of Memphis has experienced the opposite phenomenon: Online courses have pass rates above, and failure and withdrawal rates below, students in on-campus courses. These figures present a situation where retention data for online courses are not as bad as some may think and may improve in the future as experience with designing and delivering online courses is gained.

However, retention rates in online courses can and should surely improve. But how is this to be accomplished? Fortunately, the research literature on campus-based education has thoroughly explored several retention theories—such as Tinto (1987, 1998), Bean and Metzner (1985), and Astin (1977, 1984, 1993a)—and documented evidence of how and when these theories help improve retention rates. These theories proposed, and found ample evidence for, the importance of getting students engaged in their collegiate surroundings—from participating in student organizations to engaging in conversations with faculty or becoming vitally interested in their studies—which encourages students to stay enrolled and get their degrees.

Definitions

However, before reviewing the early literature around engagement, two definitions are needed to clarify the topics in this monograph.

Online Learning

The history of student learning using the Internet has generated multiple terms for the phenomenon. Online learning has been referred to as a type of distance education and as web-based learning, e-learning, and online education. Its definition is further confused by referring to discrete portions of a traditional, face-to-face, or on-campus class conducted online; a hybrid or blended class that uses both face-to-face and online learning techniques; and an all-online course. Things are made more confusing when online learning is an online program, wherein a full degree program is offered through online courses. Unfortunately, writers often use the term they are most familiar with or that their campus prefers, so terms used in specific studies may be different although they refer to similar instructional structures.

For this monograph, "online learning" refers most often to the fully online course that has been designed to be offered over the Internet and uses web-based materials and activities (grading, discussions) made possible by various course management systems or other software packages. However, when discussing specific studies or authors, the term used in the given article or report is used to be consistent with the original author. The monograph also includes research conducted on blended models if the findings are pertinent to student engagement in the online portions of the class.

Engagement

Kuh (2009) defines engagement in this way: "The engagement premise is straightforward and easily understood: the more students study a subject, the more they know about it, and the more students practice and get feedback from faculty and staff members on their writing and collaborative problem solving, the deeper they come to understand what they are learning" (p. 5). This definition emphasizes how engagement results when the student's involvement in learning (such as participating in a discussion or collaborating on solving problems) contributes to their learning and sustains their further involvement in course activities. The activities that have been found to be engaging in online learning are the focus of this monograph.

The Basis for Student Engagement on Campus

Early research on college student outcomes benefited from Astin's (1984, 1999) theory of involvement, which proposes that students learn more when they are involved in various academic and social aspects of the college experience. In other words, the more students engage in academic activities, participate in campus activities, and/or interact with faculty, the more they develop the skills and confidence to complete their education. This theory was based on Pace's (1980) "quality of effort" concept that captured the student's effort to use various college offerings (such as facilities and library resources) and led to several studies on the impact of student effort on retention and graduation (see Pascarella & Terenzini, 1991, 2005, for reviews of this literature). Early research studies also led to the development of Chickering and Gamson's (1987) Seven Principles for Good Practice in Undergraduate Education that include: (a) student–faculty contact, (b) cooperation among students, (c) active learning, (d) prompt feedback, (e) time-on-task, (f) high expectations, and (g) respect for diverse talents and ways of learning. These principles will have clear connections to the engagement literature to be reviewed in later chapters. The principles have also been widely applied to online learning (Chickering & Ehrman, 1996), perhaps suggesting that the principles of engagement for online learning are not so different from the face-to-face classroom. Nora (2003) developed a similar Student/Institution Engagement Model that emphasizes the various interactions between student and institution that create commitment to the institution because the student comes to see that he or she belongs there and recognizes the benefit that will accrue when the degree is completed at the institution. The model has been applied to students in web-based classes, and consistent results were found to those for students enrolled in more traditional formats (Sutton & Nora, 2008–2009).

The work of these early theorists and researchers led to the development of a number of early instruments intended to capture student experiences (the CSEQ or College Student Experience Questionnaire and the CCSEQ or Community College Student Experience Questionnaire). With the growing emphasis on the concept and importance of student engagement, a new instrument was needed.

Results From the National Survey of Student Engagement (NSSE)

Although this monograph will address student engagement in online learning, it is important to recognize the role of the National Survey of Student Engagement (NSSE or "Nessie") that was developed for the study of engagement on campuses and in traditional coursework and not online learning. NSSE is built on five benchmarks, briefly described as follows (Hu & McCormick, 2012):

1. Level of academic challenge (measures the extent to which colleges emphasize student effort and set high expectations), which includes questions about how many hours per week students study and the amount of reading or writing required in the courses.
2. Active and collaborative learning (measures student engagement with learning both alone and with other students), which includes questions on asking questions in class, making presentations, and working on group projects.
3. Student–faculty interaction (measures the extent to which students interact with faculty in and out of class), which includes questions on how often students discuss ideas with faculty or work with faculty on projects.
4. Enriching educational experience (measures several educational activities), which includes questions about interactions with diverse others and participation with learning communities, service learning, internships, and research with faculty.
5. Supportive campus environment (measures the quality of student relationships with peers, faculty, and staff), which includes questions that capture students' perceptions of campus support.

The first four benchmarks can be clearly applied to the online course or program (and even a supportive campus environment can be done virtually), although specific items in the instrument may not be applicable to the online setting.

For example, depending on the specific item, NSSE-based research may be helpful in identifying engagement tactics for online learning, with some provisos, however. Although NSSE includes such items as "Discussed ideas from readings or class notes" under student–faculty interactions, it will have to be assumed that online students conduct this discussion either online or over the phone or Skype or other medium. However, under skill development, students may not be able to "speak clearly and effectively" in online courses unless, of course, a web-based system for capturing speech is used. These examples provide a useful insight into NSSE research: some items may provide a clue to possible tactics to increasing engagement in online courses, but other items may be based on a campus-based experience that assumes face-to-face instruction predominates and therefore may be less helpful to the online setting. The instrument may need to be modified so that the NSSE items apply appropriately to online learning (or develop a version of the NSSE items that specifically captures the online analogue of a campus-based activity) so that the NSSE can be helpful in identifying the level and sources of engagement for online students.

Although NSSE results are most frequently applied to traditional or on-campus students attending two- and four-year higher education institutions, a few studies have specifically looked at NSSE results for online students. For example, Robinson and Hullinger (2008) compared NSSE results for on-campus and online students and found that the online students scored higher on four benchmarks than first-year or senior students. The study also found several differences: by major (technology and management majors reported higher levels of engagement), grade point average (GPA; not surprisingly, students with A grades were higher in engagement), and age (with older students more engaged and especially in real-world discussions). These types of differences are critical when comparing NSSE scores of online to on-campus students because online programs often appeal to different kinds of students based on the content of the program. For example, many online programs prepare or upgrade professional skills and therefore appeal to adult, working professionals, and other online programs are directed toward teaching more basic skills as in general education coursework at a community college and may appeal to younger, more traditional-age students. In other words, to the extent that NSSE results can be broken down to capture subgroup differences, they are more valuable for helping an individual online program understand how well it engages students and improve its engagement strategies for the future.

Chen, Lambert, and Guidry (2010) used NSSE data to tell a different story about engagement for students using various types of technologies (the sample included students who were in web-only, blended, and face-to-face classes and various combinations thereof). The results suggested that even after controlling for a number of individual and institutional characteristics, a positive correlation was found between the use of technology and measures of engagement. This finding is consistent with prior studies using NSSE data to explore technology issues (Hu & Kuh, 2001; Kuh & Hu, 2001; Nelson Laird & Kuh, 2005). In other words, some use of technology may have a positive impact on engagement.

In a study using the Community College Survey of Student Engagement (CCSSE) that includes items developed for online study, the students in web-only courses were less engaged than students in blended classes (Fisher, 2010). However, the lack of engagement was attributed less to the online setting and more to students not experiencing active and collaborative pedagogies, interacting one-on-one with faculty, or experiencing social and academic support. Fisher (2010) is an excellent introduction to the contents of this monograph because it clarifies that the problem of engagement (or learning or retention) cannot be attributed solely or exclusively to the online setting, but to the lack of appropriate pedagogical choices that include the kind of learning activities that seem to encourage student engagement in online learning.

Importance of Online Learning

Online learning has become one of many tactics that higher education institutions have adopted to address the many challenges of static budgets, increasing access, and improving productivity. Enrollments in online courses and programs have exploded in the past two decades, growing to 6.7 million students in fall 2011 (Allen & Seaman, 2012); this is approximately 30% of all higher education enrollments in fall 2011 (NCES, 2012). Indeed, research conducted by Allen and Seaman (2012) on 2,820 higher education institutions found that 32% of all higher education students take at least one online course. This means that the collegiate environment for many students is online. These students are not only enrolled in the online course or online degree program, but they are participating in a wide range of web-based academic and student services that support both online and on-campus students. In other words, the online experiences of students can and do matter a great deal and can help higher education institutions improve in ways sought by society at large. Therefore, finding ways for online students to become and stay engaged in their courses and educational programs is important.

Online students are no longer an amorphous and unclear group that institutions may not know about or understand. Aslanian and Clinefelter (2013) surveyed 1,500 online students and found that 65% and 72% agreed completely that their online education was a worthwhile financial and time investment, respectively. Most were undergraduates (with 13% earning certificates, 3% working on licensure, 21% working on associate's degrees, and 27% on bachelor's degrees), but graduate students were also well represented (32% were enrolled in master's degree programs and 4% in doctoral programs). Business is the most popular degree program at the undergraduate and graduate levels, only 5% have tried MOOCs (Massively Open Online Courses) and 4% enrolled in one but dropped out, 65% are in not-for-profit institutions, and 47% are enrolled in an online program offered by an institution relatively close to them or less than 50 miles away. More interestingly, many are dedicated online students: 44% indicated that they did not consider enrolling in hybrid or campus-based programs. They are experienced as well: 44% had taken an online course before. Students choose learning online due to the flexibility it offers and the need to manage multiple responsibilities. These students are also predominantly older: 56% of all distance education students in 2007–2008 were over age 24 (NCES, 2011b). In other words, these are primarily adult students who are interested in learning online, choose online programs for particular reasons, and are likely to know what they are getting into.

Relevance of Monograph

The focus of this monograph is to review the theories and published research about student engagement in online learning and address a number of questions about student engagement that are particularly relevant to several audiences. First, faculty will be interested in learning new techniques for improving student engagement in their online courses, testing some of the techniques, and sharing their results with their peers in published research articles or conference presentations. Second, course designers (who certainly may include faculty) will also be interested in learning which techniques have been studied and what results have been documented so that they may choose the most effective or appropriate engagement technique in online courses. Third, academic leaders—who may be at the chair, dean, provost, or presidential level—may wish to learn more about engagement in the online setting so they can help online programs increase student engagement, learning, and retention. Fourth, those leaders directly responsible for online learning operations—be they in Continuing Education or Extended Programs—may find some of these techniques and research findings worth sharing with the faculty and program directors of online programs. Lastly, students of online learning—be they graduate students or instructors who wish to improve what they do—will be interested in reviewing the state-of-the-art research on student engagement in the online setting and perhaps undertake future studies that will develop our understanding of how to do online learning well.

Please note that the terms "faculty" and "instructors" are used throughout this monograph in a largely interchangeable fashion. However, if the original study being discussed referred to faculty, then that term is used. If the discussion is more general and would apply to instructors at all levels (including the community college and university), then the more inclusive term is used.

Also, the emphasis of this monograph is on the pedagogies, activities, and learning theories that impact student engagement in online learning rather than on specific technologies or software programs or web applications. The intent is to provide readers with instruction-based guidance not tied to a specific product that may soon be replaced by a new technology or program.

Organization of Monograph

Rather than conduct a review of research by topic, this review of research is approached as if an instructor or course designer were asking questions about what works and why. Each chapter begins with a question that is answered as thoroughly as present research knowledge allows.

The second chapter answers the question, "What theories help explain student engagement in online learning?" The chapter presents several theories and explains their importance to engagement in the online setting, whether the theories were developed for online learning or more traditional forms of education.

The third chapter answers the question, "What techniques for student engagement should be considered by the online course designer or instructor?" This chapter is the longest chapter as it first presents basic strategies based on the early work of Moore (1989, 1990), who stressed the importance of interaction of certain types (with faculty, content, and other students). Then the chapter presents a range of pedagogical approaches for achieving student engagement in online learning, grouping them by type, and discussing the research done on them.

The fourth chapter answers the question, "What effects have been found for online student engagement?" It presents the research that has been done that specifically investigates the impact of engagement on a variety of outcomes. Given the state of this literature, the chapter will also outline the kinds of research that need to be done in the future to better understand what can be gained by deploying various engagement techniques.

The fifth chapter answers the question, "Are there limits to student engagement?" This section discusses the reasons why some problems may never be overcome by the engagement efforts of higher education institutions and why 100% engagement, or 100% retention, may be unachievable or highly unlikely.

The sixth chapter answers the question, "What can we conclude about how to increase student engagement in online learning?" This final chapter attempts to summarize the findings across all of the chapters into general propositions about student engagement online and outline the remaining research questions that need attention by researchers interested in studying student engagement in online learning.

The monograph is organized to push the analysis of engagement in online settings from a more general and theoretical basis to more specific and research-based insights. Readers needing different types of information (relevant theories of instruction, research results, and specific engagement tactics) can find useful information in a particular chapter. Therefore, a certain amount of repetition is built into the approach as later chapters are built upon the material in earlier chapters.

This monograph is intended to provide specific approaches to increase student engagement in online learning, and also provide broad advice about what works and why so that new ideas may be assessed against these early findings. If this monograph is successful, it will invite a new generation of researchers to the study of online learning, and energize instructors, designers, and institutional leaders to adopt, test, and improve upon what the field knows about student engagement and online learning.

Summary

This chapter provided an overview of the various challenges facing colleges and universities that explains why online learning has been adopted by many higher education institutions as a way to increase access and improve productivity. After a short review of engagement theory and the NSSE instrument, it becomes clear why student engagement in online learning has been promoted as a way to increase student retention in online coursework, which can help institutions produce more college graduates. However, engagement in online learning focuses more on what is happening in the course or degree program than all of the activities or services offered by an institution.

Learning Theories and Student Engagement

Overview

THEORIES EXPLAIN WHAT HAPPENS and why it happens, and learning theories generate educational practices and the improvement of practice. Indeed, it is true that "There is nothing more practical than a good theory" (Lewin, 1952, p. 169). Learning theories underpin how traditional face-to-face and online courses are designed and therefore indicate how online learning can improve in the future. Therefore, theories are critical to understanding how students learn online and how they engage in their learning. Learning theories are the beginning point for the journey to understand student engagement in online learning.

This chapter will answer the question, "Which learning theories explain student engagement?" and especially student engagement in online learning. The focus will be identifying learning theories that have been studied in online learning research or have a connection to research on student engagement in the face-to-face classroom. It begins with an extensive discussion of the Community of Inquiry (CoI) model, perhaps the most extensively researched model for learning online, and then proceeds to other theories such as constructivism, experiential and active learning, authentic learning, transformational learning, and the role of community online.

FIGURE 1
The CoI Model

Source: https://coi.athabascau.ca/coi-model/. Reprinted with permission.

Community of Inquiry

This chapter will first review the CoI model (Garrison, Anderson, & Archer, 2000), the first learning model developed specifically and solely for online learning.

The Basic Model

The CoI model (summarized in Figure 1) posits that learning is the result of three overlapping "presences": teaching presence, social presence, and cognitive presence. Each of these presences was based on prior learning theories. For example, cognitive presence was based on Dewey (1910) and constructivism. Dewey (1910) stressed the role of community and inquiry where inquiry occurs in an interpersonal environment (see Garrison, Anderson, & Archer, 2010, for a history of the development of the CoI). Cognitive presence recasts Dewey's phases of reflective thought and problem solution into four steps: triggering event, exploration, integration, and resolution (Garrison, Anderson, & Archer, 2010).

The Community of Inquiry (CoI) Instrument

Garrison et al. (2000) pioneered an instrument for capturing elements of the three presences that has been tested in different online settings and with different types of students enrolled in different disciplines and institutional types. (Details on the validation processes can be found in Arbaugh et al. [2008].) Several studies have used factor analysis to confirm that the instrument produces three factors (or presences), where individual items on the instrument (see next) load onto the appropriate factor (Arbaugh, 2013; Díaz, Swan, Ice, & Kupczynski, 2010; Garrison, Cleveland-Innes, & Fung, 2010) or presence (see also Arbaugh et al., 2008; Bangert, 2009). Other factor analyses have found that teaching presence loads onto two separate factors (Arbaugh et al., 2008) that capture how the presence occurs over time (the instructor's design of the class before it is offered and the instructor's facilitation and instruction while the class is underway). In a study of over 2000 online students, Shea and Bidjerano (2009) found that the three factors explained 63% of the variance in student responses.

To understand the CoI, the specific items that comprise the components of each presence captured in the CoI instrument (Version 14) should be reviewed (Table 1). Each item is answered in a five-point Likert format, where 1 = strongly disagree, 2 = disagree, 3 = neutral, 4 = agree, and 5 = strongly agree.

Different studies have assessed the role and impact of the presences (and the multiple elements that comprise each presence) on student learning. What has been interesting to monitor as this research progressed is both how universal the concepts are (how they apply to online coursework in many disciplines and with students at many levels) and how the presences work together and separately to create an engaging and effective student learning experience. Research has found that the three presences do interconnect and influence each other as hypothesized in the model (Garrison, Cleveland-Innes, & Fung, 2010).

The CoI model proposes that engagement in learning as well as the learning itself is the result of a well-designed and facilitated online course (teaching presence), interaction with course content and other students focused on learning (social presence), and focused problem exploration and resolution

TABLE 1
CoI Instrument

Teaching Presence

Design and Organization

1. The instructor clearly communicated important course topics.
2. The instructor clearly communicated important course goals.
3. The instructor provided clear instructions on how to participate in course learning activities.
4. The instructor clearly communicated important due dates/time frames for learning activities.

Facilitation

5. The instructor was helpful in identifying areas of agreement and disagreement on course topics that helped me to learn.
6. The instructor was helpful in guiding the class toward understanding course topics in a way that helped me clarify my thinking.
7. The instructor helped to keep course participants engaged and participating in productive dialogue.
8. The instructor helped keep the course participants on task in a way that helped me to learn.
9. The instruction encouraged course participants to explore new concepts in this course.
10. Instructor actions reinforced the development of a sense of community among course participants.

Direct Instruction

11. The instructor helped to focus discussion on relevant issues in a way that helped me to learn.
12. The instructor provided feedback that helped me understand my strengths and weaknesses.
13. The instructor provided feedback in a timely fashion.

Social Presence

Affective Expression

14. Getting to know other course participants gave me a sense of belonging in the course.
15. I was able to form distinct impressions of some course participants.
16. Online or web-based communication is an excellent medium for social interaction.

Open Communication

17. I felt comfortable conversing through the online medium.
18. I felt comfortable participating in the course discussions.
19. I felt comfortable interacting with other course participants.

Group Cohesion

20. I felt comfortable disagreeing with other course participants while still maintaining a sense of trust.

(Continued)

TABLE 1
Continued

21. I felt that my point of view was acknowledged by other course participants.
22. Online discussions help me to develop a sense of collaboration.

Cognitive Presence

Triggering Event
23. Problems posed increased my interest in course issues.
24. Course activities piqued my curiosity.
25. I felt motivated to explore content-related questions.

Exploration
26. I utilized a variety of information sources to explore problems posed in this course.
27. Brainstorming and finding relevant information helped me resolve content-related questions.
28. Online discussions were valuable in helping me appreciate different perspectives.

Integration
29. Combining new information helped me answer questions raised in course activities.
30. Learning activities helped me construct explanations/solutions.
31. Reflection on course content and discussions helped me understand fundamental concepts in this class.

Resolution
32. I can describe ways to test and apply the knowledge created in this course.
33. I have developed solutions to course problems that can be applied in practice.
34. I can apply the knowledge created in this course to my work or other non-class-related activities.

Source: https://coi.athabascau.ca/coi-model/coi-survey. Reprinted with permission.

(cognitive presence). By designing an online course to maximize the three presences, the instructor can ensure that interaction, active engagement, and student learning result (Garrison & Cleveland-Innes, 2005; Swan, Matthews, Bogle, Boles, & Day, 2012). But mere interaction is not sufficient; it must be interaction that promotes and supports students' deep engagement and critical reflection on the issues of the course.

Research on the Community of Inquiry Model

The CoI is now a well-researched model (Boston et al., 2009; Díaz et al., 2010; Meyer, 2003, 2004a; Shea & Bidjerano, 2009; Swan, 2001, among many others) and one that is popular in research on online learning. That makes the model—and the findings resulting from its use—important to understanding the factors that affect student engagement. For example, early research on *cognitive presence* found that students seemed to stay at the exploration level rather than move on to the integration and resolution phases of the discussion (Garrison et al., 2000; Kanuka & Anderson, 1998; Meyer, 2003); based on these early studies, it became clear that student progression through all four stages of cognitive presence did not always or naturally occur (this finding has been duplicated using a different model than the CoI; see Fahy, Crawford, & Ally, 2001). In another study, students indulged in "serial monologues" (each student posting to the discussion board but not connecting their post to prior postings of other students) rather than collaboration and progression through the four stages of cognitive presence (Pawan, Paulus, Yalcin, & Chang, 2003). Movement through all four stages of cognitive presence must be embedded in the goals of the assignment, with explicit instruction to students that they should purposefully go through the four stages: from the "triggering question," to "exploration" and then "integration," and finishing with a resolution (or several resolutions) to the problem posed in the initial "triggering question." Or students need to be told that they should produce practical applications that the group determines can solve the proposed problems (Arnold & Ducate, 2006); only when the instructor designed tasks that focused on problem solving do learners move through the four stages to a final resolution (Murphy, 2004). Clearly, the teacher plays a decisive role in student learning when he or she selects a particular activity; for example, webquests (an inquiry-based assignment where answers can be found on the web) produced high levels of cognitive presence in online discussions while using invited experts produced low levels (Kanuka, Rourke, & Laflamme, 2007); one explanation for this result is that webquests require active engagement in searching the web and listening to experts may elicit a more passive student response. In other words, the role that the instructor plays in designing the assignment and providing guidance to students about what is expected in a particular assignment (aspects of teaching presence) supports the development of problem-solving skills (cognitive presence) that in turn contributes to the student's educational experience.

The essential interplay and mutual support of teaching and social presence is extended by Archibald (2010), who found that the teaching and social presences explained approximately 69% of the variance in cognitive presence even after students' learning readiness, prior online learning experience, and prior collaborative learning experience were controlled. This is a powerful explanation for why teaching presence—which captures the design of the assignment, communication of goals to students, and ongoing instructor input into the course as it proceeds—influences how well students move through the four levels of cognitive presence as noted earlier.

Social presence (Rourke, Anderson, Garrison, & Archer, 2001) is colloquially conceived as the perception that real people are behind the online communications posted to a discussion board. Some researchers have investigated a variety of means for projecting one's presence; for example, digital storytelling (Lowenthal & Dunlap, 2010) or posting a video of the instructor to the online course made him or her more real, present, or familiar to the online student (Borup, West, & Graham, 2012). A sense of social presence also contributes to individuals speaking freely and comfortably in a discussion as well as revealing one's personality to others.

Social presence relates to student satisfaction (Benbunan-Fich & Hiltz, 2003) and learning outcomes (Arbaugh, 2005). However, several authors have questioned its importance. For example, affective indicators of social presence decline, whereas aspects of group cohesion increase over the duration of a course (Shea et al., 2010). Social presence may be less necessary in a cohort-model program, where students know each other from classes in prior terms, so that reestablishing social connections need be done only when it has been several weeks since students last met online. Garrison and Arbaugh (2007) may be capturing this phenomenon when they indicate that social presence becomes "transparent" as a course progresses and as students move from getting to know each other to focusing on academic tasks together. Students confirm this interpretation; when asked what items on the CoI instrument were most important, they deemed social presence to be the least important with cognitive presence ranked next highest in importance and teaching presence as most important (Díaz et al., 2010).

Teaching presence is necessary, especially the items (see list of items within the instrument mentioned in Table 1) related to designing a good instructional experience prior to the course being offered and being supportive of learning while the course is in session (Swan et al., 2012). It also causally influences both social and cognitive presences (Shea & Bidjerano, 2009). In fact, "student perception of teaching presence predicted a significant direct effect on perceptions of cognitive presence" (Garrison, Cleveland-Innes, & Fung, 2010, p. 34) that captures students' perceptions of how one presence affects their own learning. As for different disciplines, Arbaugh (2013) has explored how direct instruction may need to be emphasized when teaching in a "hard" discipline, where students expect instructors to provide content; this finding indicates a need for more studies of how individual items of each presence—or the presences as a whole—are valued differently in various disciplines.

Teaching presence plays a central role in students' online learning experiences as it provides structure (design) and leadership (facilitation and direct instruction) to the class. *Facilitation* includes the instructor identifying shared meaning as well as areas of agreement and disagreement, and pushing students toward consensus; *direct instruction* involves the instructor evaluating discussions for accurate understanding, providing opportunities for students to scaffold knowledge, and providing new and relevant sources for the group's consideration. Facilitation and direct instruction produce a high level of social presence for the instructor as well as instructor immediacy, or the sense that an instructor is involved in the course (Arbaugh, 2001; Richardson & Swan, 2003). But advice on how much day-to-day presence is needed in the online course on the part of the instructor is less consistent. Vaughan (2004) found that the more the instructor dominates the discussion through the posting of direct instruction comments, the fewer facilitation comments are made that can impact the movement of students through the four phases of cognitive presence. Perhaps for younger or novice students having a constant instructional presence is helpful, but Arbaugh (2010) found that the average amount of time spent per login by the instructor was a negative predictor of student learning. This issue will be taken up more thoroughly in the third chapter. In any case, the CoI model has been and should continue to be used to explore how, when, and how much teacher presence in a course is necessary and when it is not.

Impact on Engagement, Retention, and Community

CoI-based research explains other important outcomes such as student engagement (Nagel & Kotzé, 2010) as well as student learning (Rovai, 2002b; Shea, 2006; Shea, Li, & Pickett, 2006), student satisfaction (Arbaugh, 2001; Swan, 2001), and sense of community (Garrison & Arbaugh, 2007). Its primary influence on engagement is through the assigning of engaging tasks (a function of teaching presence) that requires them to move through the four stages of cognitive presence as they attempt to solve the problem presented or complete the project assigned. The field needs more studies that specifically prove whether and how specific use of the CoI during the design and operation of an online course impacts student engagement, although it is fair to assume that all three presences play a role in engaging students in their own learning.

Research using the CoI also indicates a relationship to retention in online courses and programs (Meyer, 2012a; Meyer, Bruwelheide, & Poulin, 2006). When courses were redesigned using the CoI, Vaughan (2010) found that the retention rate climbed to 100%. In Meyer (2012a), research investigating the impact on retention of using the CoI model to help design and conduct online courses was reviewed, and then the separate elements of the CoI model were integrated within several existing retention theories developed prior to the Internet—including Tinto (1987, 1998), Bean and Metzner (1985), and Metzner and Bean (1987)—as well as retention theories developed for online coursework (Berge & Huang, 2004; Rovai, 2003). The final model proposes that any effect on retention that the CoI may have is through an intermediating variable (here called student learning in the course). However, retention can also be affected by a range of external factors (such as family support, finances, work responsibilities, and life crises), academic factors (such as student ability and course demands), social factors (such as peer or teacher interaction and involvement in campus groups or events), and other factors (such as transfer credit policies and changes in major). The model, which requires testing and modification by researchers into online education and retention, appears in Figure 2.

FIGURE 2
Proposed Model Connecting CoI, Learning, and Retention

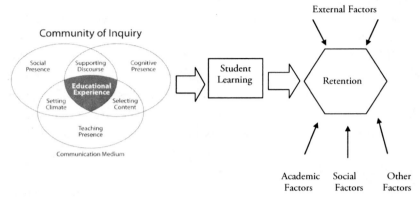

Source: Meyer (2012a, p. 332). Reprinted by permission of the publisher.

Future Developments

As the CoI has been studied, several researchers have proposed additions or changes to the CoI. "Learning presence" has been proposed to better explain effective learner behavior in fully online courses, especially behaviors dealing with complex learning activities and collaborative efforts (Shea et al., 2012). Learning presence requires forethought and planning, monitoring, and strategizing that are conceptually part of "self-regulating" behaviors that help learners succeed in particular situations such as debates or collaborative projects. These self-regulating behaviors are thought to be different from those included in the three presences. Learning self-regulation is especially important in online learning because successful learning online depends upon the student's discipline, self-direction, and ability to remain motivated. Learning presence may be particularly relevant for developing and identifying engagement in students, because it requires effort on the part of the student (e.g., planning, monitoring, and strategizing) that may generate commitment to learning or completing assignments. The revised CoI including learning presence (see Figure 3) is conceptualized as providing a separate and coordinated influence (along with social presence and teaching presence) on cognitive presence.

FIGURE 3
CoI Model With Learning Presence Represented

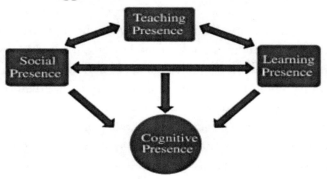

Suggestion for a Revised CoI Model

Teaching Presence · Social Presence · Learning Presence · Cognitive Presence

Source: Shea et al. (2012, p. 93). Reprinted by permission of the publisher.

Another intriguing development for the CoI is the assessment of metacognition in an online learning environment. Metacognition is a "higher-order, executive process that monitors and coordinates other cognitive processes engaged during learning" (Tobias & Everson, 2009, p. 108). Perhaps contrary to one's immediate assumptions of a solely internal process, metacognition is thought to be socially situated, requiring the presence of a community so that metacognition can develop and manifest within the individual. It involves knowledge of cognition (or awareness of the self as a learner), monitoring of cognition (reflection on thinking and learning and changes in one's thinking), and regulation (enacting and controlling the learning process) of cognition (Akyol & Garrison, 2011). Garrison and Arbaugh (2007) proposed that metacognition is not only evident in cognitive presence, but is created by teaching presence as instructors help students recognize their own thinking and how it changes as the discussion progresses or the assignment is undertaken and completed. Based on analyses of discussion postings, Akyol and Garrison (2011) identified when and how often evidence of these metacognitive dimensions was found. Although knowledge of cognition appeared the least, monitoring of cognition and regulation of cognition occurred in 35.8–60.5% of the discussions and seemed to increase as the class progressed. It makes sense at this juncture to suppose that these metacognitive functions can and do require engagement in learning on the part of the student, as he or she explains, questions, clarifies, justifies, or strategizes what is known, what is to be learned, and how to accomplish it.

It is difficult to know whether the concepts of learning presence or metacognition are the same or different; however, both concepts deal with self-regulation of the student's thinking and learning. It is perhaps premature to state whether these concepts will be proven feasible to measure and important to learning online, but they appear to identify an important conceptual area for future researchers to explore.

A final development is the movement of coding of online discussions from the prevalent use of content analysis that relies on subjective classifications to a quantitative content analysis technique (Rourke & Anderson, 2004). A movement to quantitative analysis will help research on online discussions (a popular area of research in the early years) move from a descriptive to an inferential mode and from reliance on a few coders (often only one person, the researcher) to a validated coding protocol.

Constructivist Learning

Constructivism assumes that learning occurs when the student is interacting with others (known as social constructivism) or is actively engaged with a task or course content or interacting with the environment. It depends upon what students already know, the kinds of experiences they have had in the past, and how they have organized their knowledge. It emphasizes that individuals construct knowledge and that learning is an active and not passive endeavor. Constructivism is dependent upon engagement, and perhaps all engagement research implies a belief in constructivist learning theory. In any case, constructivism is contrasted with prior learning theories that proposed that an expert could ensure learning by telling or lecturing a group of students and that this would result in the expert's learning being transferred in whole or in part to the student. In an intriguing assessment of student orientation—constructivist or objectivist (where truths are absolute and learning depends on receiving content from the instructor)—differences were found based on students' age (Akyol, Ice, Garrison, & Mitchell, 2010). Younger (18–22 years old) and older (48–62 years old) students were more objectivist, treating instructor goals for the course as synonymous with cognitive outcomes; other age groups (23–37 and 38–47) were more aligned with the position that knowledge is constructed, largely as a result of their work experiences. These findings make clear that while emphasis on a constructivist teaching philosophy may be currently in vogue, students have different expectations of what teaching and learning is and whether it will be based on their prior experiences in school or work.

In a study of online discussions, Kanuka and Anderson (1998) found evidence that when contradictions occurred, new knowledge was occasionally crafted. This captures the state of "cognitive dissonance," where new information contradicts existing beliefs, thereby creating a state of tension or discomfort. New information must be accommodated or ignored to relieve the tension. This research emphasizes both the need and role of introducing discord of some kind to the online discussion so that new knowledge can be constructed.

However, for online discussions to be productive, the instructor may need to establish a level for the discussion to operate at; once established in the "triggering question" posed to an online discussion, subsequent postings were primarily at the same level (Meyer, 2005). For example, if asked knowledge questions, the subsequent discussion stayed at that level and infrequently rose to higher levels. Similarly, online discussions work best educationally when they are given an objective, such as "resolve this contradiction" or "if this information is true, what does it mean for our knowledge?"

Constructivist learning can also be fruitfully applied to faculty development and/or changing faculty views of teaching and learning. Gallini and Barron (2001/2002) found that when faculty members new to the web used it in their courses, 70% of them stated that they had changed the way they approached teaching. This finding presages the studies on transformative learning, which follow.

Experiential Learning and Active Learning

Based on the definition of constructivism mentioned earlier, experiential learning is a type of constructivist learning that draws upon the student doing and reflecting upon what was done and how. Based on what is done or its setting, it has also been called active learning, cooperative learning, and service learning. Its theoretical basis was provided by Kolb (1984), who proposed that learning went through four stages: from concrete experience, to reflective observation, to abstract conceptualization, and to active experimentation. The cycle repeats as new concrete experience is gained, reflected upon, generalized into an abstract concept, and then actively tested or experimented with in a new setting.

Active and experiential learning uses case studies, simulations, role playing, and debates, all of which can be accommodated within the online course. All of these instructional methods depend upon the student becoming actively involved in their own learning, either through a physical activity, joint assignment with others, researching information, or engaging in multiple points of view. For example, when Schrand (2008) redesigned a traditional assignment using multimedia, it provided more opportunity for students to become involved, greater discussion and reflection on the part of students resulted, and increased student engagement was the result. When project-based learning (which is oriented to students solving a problem and often results in a product of some kind) was used in online classes, it produced higher levels of knowledge construction, including the evaluation of ideas and crafting of solutions (Koh, Herring, & Hew, 2010), than in non-project-based classes. Williams and Chinn (2009) found a similar result when more active, technology-based activities were used, and Peters, Shmerling, and Karren (2011) also found that male students with a preference for active experimentation experienced greater engagement in online coursework.

Authentic Learning

Experiential learning can certainly include authentic learning situations, because authentic learning stresses the use of real situations. These may be tied to the student's chosen career or current events. Herrington, Oliver, and Reeves (2003) presented several characteristics of authentic activities, including "ill-defined" and "complex," but also requiring multiple perspectives, the opportunity to collaborate, make choices, and reflect on learning. One can see from this set of characteristics that authentic learning both requires student engagement in understanding and solving the problem, and encourages them to go deeper into the learning task. However, not all students appreciate having these responsibilities placed on them, and they may reject the task. Herrington et al. (2003) stresses the importance of encouraging engagement in the authentic task by purposefully encouraging the "willing suspension of disbelief." Originally coined by Coleridge and applied to the reading of poetry, this phrase also applies to treating the authentic task as if it were real, and not an educational exercise.

Transformational Learning

Transformative learning has its roots in Mezirow's (1991) theory of adult education that emphasizes how adults choose to learn what is important and applicable to their lives. It has been applied to traditional, face-to-face classes, but is also increasingly used in online coursework that depends on students' working through their disorienting dilemmas. Such dilemmas present information contradictory to students' existing beliefs, thereby encouraging students to seek additional information as they evaluate those beliefs, which often results in personal and/or intellectual growth. To do this, Merriam (2004) noted that students must have a certain level of cognitive development, involving both critical reflection but also rational discourse on the dilemma, one's beliefs, and alternatives. The process presumes both individual effort and group effort in the discussion.

As Meyers (2008) contends, "Internet courses are well suited to transformative pedagogy" (p. 219). This involves the faculty person creating trust among class members and faculty, finding ways to present disorienting dilemmas effectively, and supporting students in their examination of assumptions and imagining alternatives. This can be done by one student working alone or with a group of students; examples of pedagogical approaches fitted to this learning theory are debates, blogs, and wikis that have as their purpose creating dilemmas and encouraging transformative learning. Meyers (2008) also urges the use of real-world problems that deal with inequities to help individuals develop new views that may be based on multiple philosophical perspectives (e.g., psychological, sociological, and economic). Transformative learning approaches have also been adopted by faculty developers who were responsible for helping faculty learn how to teach online (McQuiggan, 2012; Meyer & Murrell, 2014); McQuiggan (2012) provided an excellent example of an action research study based on reflection journals and interviews with participants after an extensive faculty development experience. By including activities specifically intended to encourage reflection on core teaching beliefs, faculty examined their reliance on lecturing, revised assignments to emphasize student construction of knowledge, and even changed their teaching practices in face-to-face classes. These processes based on transformative learning encouraged faculty to question their prior beliefs about being the provider of content through lecture and to develop a new teaching role that emphasizes creating environments for learning.

Online Community

Although not an accepted theory of learning, the concept of online community has been a topic of research in online learning for many years and has developed a body of research worth including in this section. From the early days of online education, the development of community in an online setting has been the focus of many researchers. Community was deemed essential in online settings as a way to overcome a perceived sense of distance among students resulting from not being able to see each other or interact in ways they had been accustomed to in face-to-face classes. Palloff and Pratt (1999) laid the groundwork on this topic, which has been well researched since then. Palloff and Pratt (1999) encouraged the development of several activities or pedagogies for the online course, which taken together indicate that an online community is forming:

- *Active interaction* involving both course content and personal communication;
- *Collaborative learning* evidenced by comments among students rather than between student and instructor;
- *Socially constructed meaning* evidenced by agreement or questioning;
- *Sharing of resources* among students; and
- *Expressions of support and encouragement* exchanged between students.

Several studies have focused on the development of a community online and have found that a sense of community can be created (Rovai, 2002a; Thompson & MacDonald, 2005). One can see that several of the pedagogies in Palloff and Pratt's (1999) list are also mentioned in the context of encouraging engagement (as in active learning and collaborative learning), which indicates that creating community may be an outcome of these learning theories.

Although building online community may share some ideas (such as active interaction and socially constructed meaning) with the CoI model, the CoI is focused on the educational experience and student learning, and the CoI instrument incorporates more elements than just creating community. This shift is not a subtle one; in its early stages, social presence was considered to be fundamental to the creation of community online and it was interpreted as the need of all students for social interactions. However, Garrison (2011) subsequently reconceptualized social presence as less socializing and more social interaction around or for a learning purpose. This is consistent with the claim that "social climate" in an online class is the result of students practicing three types of social behavior: strictly social behavior, content-related communications, and functional communications (as in arranging a plan of action for a group activity; Oren, Mioduser, & Nachmias, 2002). In other words, socializing may be only one approach to the creation of community; community needs an educational goal as well.

As an example of the overlapping of community and other engagement approaches, Zach and Agosto (2009) used collaboration and knowledge sharing among students to develop a sense of community among online students. Conrad (2002a, 2002b) found that adult online students established community as a pragmatic step toward completing course tasks; although some students tolerated some social talk, not all did. They found ways to "be nice," thereby creating a modest level of community in the class. In contrast, Wegerif (1998) felt that the ability to construct a sense of community among students influenced student success or failure in the course. But LaPointe and Reisetter (2008) found similar results to Conrad (2002a, 2002b) above; although some students found the virtual community helpful to their learning, others thought the peer discussions were superfluous and inconvenient and did not support their learning. In other words, the creation of community for a social purpose may not be desired by all students, especially those with other life demands, and may be perceived by students as counterproductive to learning. The problem is that it is impossible to satisfy everyone in the class. Such findings ought to encourage instructors to seriously evaluate their students, group activities, and learning objectives before presuming that developing community around social activities is always a necessary goal or support to online learners.

Unfortunately, "community" is used in other important concepts that are different from the online community discussed earlier, which can cause confusion. Therefore, one needs to distinguish clearly between the concept of community (whether online or not) and learning communities. Learning communities have become popularized on many higher education campuses as an approach to address the needs for community and interdisciplinary learning of first-time freshmen. Learning communities were organized as a deliberate linking of courses or cluster of courses for a cohort of students (MacGregor, Smith, Tinto, & Levine, 1999). Instruction may have been conducted by team teaching and depended on interdisciplinary subjects (e.g., topics that might blend science and literature or history and social science). Students in a learning community sometimes live together in a residence hall and engage in community service. Cross (1998) found that learning communities help ameliorate attrition rates for these first-year students. Kuh (2007) called learning communities a "high-impact" engagement practice that have been found to produce students who are substantially more engaged in activities that are educationally effective compared to students not participating in such programs. This conclusion was confirmed by a study of 365 institutions where Zhao and

Kuh (2004) found that participating in a learning community was positively linked to student's engagement and satisfaction with college.

The question is whether learning communities can be conducted online. DiRamio and Wolverton (2006) surveyed attendees of a conference focused on learning communities, student learning, and student engagement. The top four items characteristic of learning communities that were proposed as applying to online learning were (a) "use group projects to promote collaborative learning," (b) "encourage students to share their own experiences and ideas in online discussions and/or postings," (c) "cluster two online classes around an interdisciplinary theme," and (d) "encourage students to take responsibility for their learning" (p. 104). Each concept provides instructors with a goal when designing and conducting coursework: (a) provide many opportunities to connect to others and ideas in the course, (b) encourage undertaking learning experiences in a real or virtual setting, and (c) encourage student motivation and empowerment for learning. These findings support the idea that learning communities can be offered through online learning, albeit with some imagination and accommodation for distant students, but may also provide a framework for collaborative learning that contributes to community in any online course.

Cognitive Engagement

Cognitive engagement is a field of research and theory of learning first defined by Corno and Mandinach (1983) as students having the ability to "learn to learn" or as "actively engaging in a variety of cognitive interpretations, including interpretations of their environments and themselves" (Richardson & Newby, 2006, p. 24). This involves both student motivations and learning strategies, such as when students find their own solutions to problems as well as learn how to learn. Richardson and Newby (2006) found that as students gained experience with online learning, they exhibited greater evidence of deep engagement in learning, evidence that they were learning to take more responsibility for their own learning (p. 32). When experienced online instructors were asked how they ensured student learning online, instructors at master's or doctoral institutions (Meyer & McNeal, 2011) and community colleges (Meyer, 2014) focused on helping students learn how to learn by focusing on providing simple tips (always log into the class each day) or more direct help (by grouping new information and scaffolding it to prior knowledge). These instructors were also very attentive to student engagement, from choosing engaging learning assignments, to using active and experiential learning, to challenging student thinking in early drafts of assignments and requiring rewrites of those assignments. Clearly, encouraging cognitive engagement is an important goal of online coursework and is an important function of online learning. Strategies to encourage cognitive engagement are the purview of the third chapter.

Transactional Distance Theory

Moore (1972, 1973) published his popular theory of transactional distance during the early days of distance education and long before the development of online learning. It was initially labeled as a theory of independent learning and teaching that included autonomous learners, distant teachers, and communication systems to connect them (Moore, 1989, 1990). The theory of transactional distance emphasizes the geographical distance between teachers and learners, but also includes educational and psychological distance as well. Transactional distance is a "psychological and communications gap, a space of potential misunderstanding between the inputs of the instructor and those of the learner" (Moore, 1991, para. 2). Such distance was thought to contribute to feelings of isolation and disconnectedness that could in turn reduce student motivation and engagement. When transactional distance is used today, the emphasis is on a gap in understanding and less on the "distance."

Transactional distance can be overcome by structure and dialogue. Structure refers to the instructional methods and strategies in the learning environment and is synonymous with choices of instructional design that include the use of appropriate pedagogies for the learning outcomes and student skill levels. Dialogue is the interaction between instructor and learner. Moore (2007) has extended this approach to include interacting with the environment (pp. 90–91), which is defined as the course learning environment or environments external to the course that are engaged in for learning purposes such as the one that might be undertaken in experiential learning or service learning.

Given its long usage, transactional distance has been widely studied (see Chen, 2001; Garrison, 2000; Lemak, Shin, Reed, & Montgomery, 2005, for a small sample of such studies). The concept continues to be used to explain what occurs in online learning, although researchers have continued to add to and revise its concepts or developed broader theories (such as the CoI) that explain more of what happens specifically in the online course. In other words, if transactional distance is characterized as simply a gap in understanding, irrespective of the medium of course delivery or geographic locations of the student and instructor, it captures an important concept that challenges all faculty and learners who are engaged in the learning process but have yet to bridge the gap in understanding between them. However, if learning is individual (and perhaps idiosyncratic) in content, then students may not learn exactly what instructors intended them to learn. In other words, those who design online coursework may need to accept that a gap in understanding may always be present when learners engage in their online courses.

Summary

What may be obvious even after this cursory review of learning theories related to student engagement is that other learning theories not yet mentioned may also impact student engagement. The theories described earlier, however, receive the most mentions in studies of student engagement and learning in the online setting. When the theories described earlier are compared—the CoI model, constructivism, experiential learning, authentic, transformative, active learning, cognitive engagement, and transactional distance—they have some similar qualities. Perhaps the strongest similarity among them is that they all stress student activity rather than passively receiving information. Activities can be with content, other students, faculty, or experiences, and they can be done alone or in a group. Using the term "activity" need not imply physical activity, but it ought to require that the student do something that can be cognitive, collaborative, or even emotional as long as it has an educational purpose. Many of these theories require that learning be relevant to the needs of that individual.

Thus, the key points from this review of learning theories are:

1. Instructional designers and instructors can use the CoI model as they design online courses to maximize social, teaching, and cognitive presence.
2. Designers and instructors need to include experiences that emphasize active learning, collaborative learning, and experiential or transformative learning.
3. Course-related experiences ought to engage students with the content, other students, and outsiders.
4. Course-related experiences ought to help create a sense of community that has an educational purpose.

Techniques for Student Engagement Online

Overview

TECHNIQUES ARE THE APPLICATIONS of theory. Techniques are the strategies, procedures, or methods that produce the desired result predicted by theory. Without them, online instructors and designers may not know precisely what they need to do to encourage student engagement. Therefore, the third chapter presents a review of the several techniques that theory predicts will produce greater student engagement. Fortunately, these techniques or strategies have often been researched, so the methods can be evaluated. A review of research on these various techniques is the next stage of the journey.

This chapter answers the question, "What techniques for student engagement should be considered by the online course designer or instructor?" It provides an overview of techniques that have been documented in research studies to improve or increase student engagement in online coursework. The chapter first reviews strategies based on the early work of Moore (1989, 1990) and then proceeds to review the research on strategies that may impact engagement with attention paid to when they work, where they work, and for whom.

The third and fourth chapters are paired in the sense that the third chapter discusses the strategies and techniques that produce engagement (the first and second columns in Figure 4) and the fourth chapter discusses research

FIGURE 4
Approach for the Third and Fourth Chapters

STRATEGIES/TECHNIQUES
Moore's interactions
Online discussions
Active/authentic learning
Instructor actions
Student preparation/skills
Instructional design
Multiple paths
Use of technologies

STUDENT
ENGAGEMENT
ONLINE

OUTCOMES

on what engagement in turn produces in terms of student outcomes (the second and third columns in Figure 4). Figure 4 displays the plan for the two chapters.

Moore's Interaction/Engagement Strategies

Research on three engagement "types" is discussed next. These engagement types are defined by Moore's (1989, 1990) essential types of interaction: student–student, student–teacher, and student–content. Moore presented one of the first popular approaches to designing distance education that is still used by many faculty who teach and develop courses for the online setting.

Student–Student

Active engagement with other students in a course (be it online or other form of distance education) has been found to be critical to learning and collaborative knowledge building (Chen & Looi, 2011; Wegerif, 1998). The forms of student–student interaction go well beyond online discussions, but can extend to group work of all kinds. And the content of student–student interaction can be of many kinds as well, from purely social, to seeking (and giving) assistance, to solving problems, and to cognitive engagement with the course content.

Student–Content

Several studies have focused on the presentation of course content and interaction of students with the content of the course. For example, Boling, Hough, Krinsky, Saleem, and Stevens (2012) interviewed students about their online learning and found that "just reading and reading and reading" (p. 120), as one student put it, provided little variation or direction to the student about what to do with the reading and depended too much on individualized learning. Disconnections—between student–student, student–instructor, and student–content—seemed to plague the design of the six online courses studied (Boling et al., 2012). Schilling (2009) found that moving content from text-only to multiple modes (visual, active, virtual) and providing multiple paths through the content improved student interaction with the content.

Student–Teacher

The role of the teacher is critical to pushing students to think more critically or deeply (Garrison & Cleveland-Innes, 2005) through guided instruction and pushing the student's understanding to deeper levels. Of course, the instructor is also critical to providing answers to the student who is confused, directions for the student who is lost, and gentle criticism when redirection is needed. Teachers provide new ways of thinking about issues, new content or readings, and new experiences to help the student acquire the learning he or she seeks.

However, instructors receive no consistent advice about their role in online discussions. Some research stresses the importance of an instructor being actively involved in the discussion, whereas other studies (Meyer & McNeal, 2011) note that teacher input often closes off discussion as students believe that the expert has spoken. Therefore, the teacher must adjust his/her involvement in a course discussion based on an assessment of the age or maturity of the students, the goals of the discussion, and an assessment of whether the instructor will help or harm learning. Younger students tend to seek reassurance of the instructor ("Is this the right answer?") and are most likely to accept the instructor's comments as gospel that will close off subsequent discussion. In other words, discussion meant to share experiences among adult professionals may need less instructor involvement than a discussion meant to challenge students to think more deeply about a topic. (These fine points of leading online discussions will be taken up later in this chapter.)

Critique

It cannot be overstated how helpful and transformative the early work of Moore was to the instructors and course developers who first took instruction online. Stressing the inclusion of the three types of interactions into the design of early distance and/or online coursework guided those early efforts and provided a framework for determining and assessing quality in terms of those interactions. However, time and experience with these interactions began to uncover some unintended problems with courses that stressed interactions with less attention to pedagogy and the educational purpose of the activity. This is not intended as a criticism of Moore, but perhaps of the modest understanding early practitioners of online learning brought to designing online courses so that interactions would result in student learning.

To some extent, early emphasis placed on interaction without being clear about an educational goal or learning objective may have inadvertently created some of the problems of poor student engagement that are outlined in more detail in the fifth chapter. Furthermore, it became clear to the field of professional online instructional designers and faculty with expertise in this area that a fourth interaction was more important, the one between student and activity.

Student–Activity

Although the three interaction types discussed earlier provided some guidance to an instructor about what to do to improve student engagement in online coursework, the Moore (1989, 1990) interaction types do not directly address pedagogy and the range of instructional activities that instructors can choose to improve student engagement as well as student learning. The interaction of student–activity (or students with a particular activity) captures two types of engagement: that of the student with a pedagogy or instructional approach (such as the use of computer games, 3D and virtual worlds, library research, and experiential learning activities) and personal preferences for engagement of that student. These two types of engagement are addressed later in the chapter. The next section will focus on exploring pedagogies and other instructional choices as well as personal learning preferences that go beyond the three interactions to engage the learner in the online learning process.

Online Discussions

Online discussions are popular opportunities for students to interact with each other, the instructor, and the course content for an instructional purpose (such as solving a problem, sharing experiences, and applying course content). In fact, the purposes that a discussion board may fulfill are limited only by the creativity and pedagogical skills of the instructor; when experienced online instructors were asked how they achieved student learning, many used the structure of online discussions but used them for functions usually reserved for focus groups, brainstorming, blogging alone or in groups, analysis of case studies, preparing a wiki, and even collaborative exams (Meyer, 2012b). Online discussion boards or similar functions are uniquely flexible tools for the online instructor. By conducting discussions via various course management systems (e.g., Blackboard and Desire2Learn) that produce a written record of what occurred, research into what does or does not happen in online discussions has exploded. As a result, online instructors and designers have better and clearer guidance on how to set up discussions to be engaging and instructionally sound. What is important in this instance is that "putting discussions online" is not sufficient guidance to instructors who want to increase student engagement and learning online; they also need to see discussions as a flexible tool that can achieve many instructional objectives: students' sharing of ideas, solving problems, reflecting on learning, and creating final products that capture learning of the individual (a blog) or a group (as in a wiki).

For example, it is important to encourage or require *early postings* in a weekly discussion, because the early posters often set the tone and direction of the discussion and are the posts read most often by all of the students. These "thought leaders" can encourage others to disagree or expand upon the early postings or they may discourage others who may feel they cannot challenge or compete with these individuals. Late postings to online discussions tend not to be read by all students and may be posted at the last minute only to satisfy a requirement for participation. Also, researchers have documented the importance of asking the *right kinds of questions to initiate* discussions (Meyer, 2004a, 2005) that emphasize the importance of *clear goals* for the discussion (such as stressing solving problems, uncovering both pros and cons to an issue, digging deeper into complex issues, or supporting statements with data or research). Meyer (2005) used Bloom's (1956) Taxonomy to analyze several online discussions; Bloom's Taxonomy classifies learning objectives as (going from more basic objectives to higher level objectives) Knowledge to Understanding to Application to Analysis to Synthesis to Evaluation. The students' posts to the discussion indicated that the level of the first triggering question that initiated the discussion largely influenced the level of student responses; for example, information-seeking questions elicited knowledge responses, but questions seeking solutions to problems elicited more creative responses at the analysis and evaluation stages. In fact, Bloom's Taxonomy has been used by other researchers (Zhu, 2006) in an effort to study online discussions and may provide novice instructors with an easily grasped framework for understanding the level of student thinking within the online discussion. Zhu (2006), Fahy et al. (2001), and Shea et al. (2010) also used *network analysis* to study online discussions to determine the types of interactions taking place; star discussions (picture a many-armed asterisk), with one individual starting and responding to the majority of messages, indicate the importance of one person, whereas interconnected web discussions (picture many asterisks connected to each other) indicate that several individuals may be sending and receiving messages. Star discussions, especially if the center is the instructor, may indicate that the instructor is dominating the discussion or exercising too much control over the agenda and direction of the discussion. Students in interconnected web networks were "more likely to exchange, elaborate on, and challenge each other's ideas" (Zhu, 2006, p. 469). These tools, among others, help instructors evaluate what happens in online classes and determine what went well and what did not. Such tools help faculty learn to develop solutions for subsequent classes that have the potential to improve future online discussions and extend their knowledge of what can be achieved through this approach.

These ideas are taken further by Garrison and Cleveland-Innes (2005). In a comparison of instructor activities across three courses, the focus was the instructor's impact on surface or deep learning. What made the difference in creating deep learning among students were teacher presence and the quality of the instructor's interaction; that is, the teacher taught, modeled, and rewarded *critical discourse*, or the serious engagement in course content through sharing and challenging ideas. For deep learning to occur, both faculty and students need to move beyond social discourse to reasoning about the content or issues included in the course. This finding again stresses providing clear guidance to students about the purpose and conduct of the discussion and then providing leadership during the discussion to stress the importance of evidence-based and logical argument. Online debates (Bender, 2003) might be one application of this finding, wherein students propose and defend ideas in a logical progression, perhaps depending on data or results from research studies to support their points. Richardson and Ice (2010) found differences in students' level of critical thinking (as captured by the four-stage cognitive presence portion of the CoI) based on which pedagogical approach was used: case-based discussion, an online debate, or open-ended discussion. A total of 78% and 77% of the posts for the case-based and debate strategies, respectively, were at the integration stage of critical thinking (the third level of cognitive presence); only 60% of the posts in the open-ended discussion reached that level. In other words, the pedagogy impacted the level of critical thinking students reached.

The work of Zhu (2006) addresses the usefulness of online discussions for encouraging cognitive engagement and uses network and content analyses to ascertain what helps or hinders students' engagement in course content. Students' efforts to critique, analyze, and synthesize course concepts or readings in online discussions are the definition of cognitive engagement for this study (Zhu, 2006). For cognitive engagement to occur, student interactions within the online discussion setting must be intentionally designed to stress student movement to deep learning, serious engagement in ideas and thinking processes, elaborating and debating ideas, and higher levels of processing (Berge, 1999; Zhu, 2006). It takes "careful planning of learning activities and facilitation" in accordance with course goals and learning objectives (Zhu, 2006, p. 471).

Active or Authentic Pedagogies

Active learning options (e.g., group work, problem solving, project work, and experiential learning) also effectively engage students in their own learning, as they do with students learning in face-to-face classrooms. A unique study of an approach that combines collaborative group learning with competition between groups—that the authors call "coopetition" (Fu, Wu, & Ho, 2009, p. 550)—found an increase in student learning attributable in part to the different types of knowledge growth that collaboration and competition engender. Collaborative learning seemed to produce higher levels of synthesis, whereas competitive learning produced higher analytic skills.

Students might undertake experiential learning projects by interviewing homeless persons to learn more about their situation and how they became homeless for an introduction to sociology course, provide active consultation with business clients for a communication program (Meyer & McNeal, 2011), or interview legislators about pressing issues for various courses, from political science to mental health or social work (Meyers, 2008). Using two national data sets to explore whether faculty made a difference in student engagement, Umbach and Wawrzynski (2005) found that higher levels of engagement resulted when faculty used active and collaborative learning and engaged students in experiences. Interestingly, several of the examples above (Meyer & McNeal, 2011; Meyers, 2008) took place outside the online classroom, but as part of an online course. Therefore, the assignment need not be conducted within the strict confines of the online course or the course management system (just as these assignments went beyond the boundaries of the traditional face-to-face classroom), but can encourage students to engage in external tasks and persons that are critical to their learning of new skills and knowledge. In fact, such assignments are limited only by the creativity and judgment of the instructor.

Some additional examples of active learning are case studies and problem-based learning, both of which can be designed to be authentic as well. Case studies need not be created in a particular model, but can be useful as long as the situation to be studied engages students in real-world situations. Paulus, Horvitz, and Shi (2006) used fictitious stories of students undertaking projects requiring teamwork whose projects sometimes went awry, that were then critiqued online by instructional design students. Engagement was evident in the students' emotional reactions to the fictitious students, and this engagement was found to be the result of the credibility and relevance of the stories to the students' experiences with their own instructional design projects. Students often brought their own past experiences to the online discussions and reflected on a range of issues that arise in teamwork. They also demonstrated an engagement in learning by applying the lessons of the stories and their discussions to their own ongoing teamwork activities. In an assessment of a campus-wide implementation of problem-based learning, the more the problem-based learning methods of instruction were used, the higher the student engagement levels became (Ahlfeldt, Mehta, & Sellnow, 2005). Combining case studies and problems may be especially powerful in engaging students in their learning.

Other active learning approaches have also been successful in encouraging student engagement online. Using problem-based learning and jigsaw groups (that divide learning among a small group of students) may also be effective engagement strategies that can be migrated from traditional sociology and nursing courses to online courses (Amador & Mederer, 2013). In Waldner, McGorry, and Widener (2010), two experimental courses in public policy and marketing management demonstrated that e-service learning (where both the instruction and the service was done 100% online) was possible, which confirms that if a type of learning was done in face-to-face settings, it may very well be transferable to the online setting.

Authentic learning is real-world-based and problem-based, and, because many employers value and encourage teamwork to solve various problems, it often includes collaborative group learning. Herrington et al. (2003) discuss this student-centered approach to learning and the problems of providing an authentic learning experience that engages learners through to completion.

(The second chapter provides a detailed description of authentic learning activities.) Meyers (2008) also stresses using real-world problems that address social and economic inequalities to expand students' understanding of the forces that affect both the individual's and societal conditions and the challenges of achieving social justice.

This review clarifies the ways in which these pedagogies can and do overlap. Active and authentic learning can be mixed effectively by using case studies that involve real-world problems; furthermore, authentic problems may require active involvement of students to resolve. Collaborative learning can involve students in solving problems or evaluating a real-world case that requires understanding of complex situations. No clear divisions among these learning approaches are necessary, so an instructor can creatively combine them in ways that increase student engagement in their online courses.

Instructor Activities

Of course, the instructor is doing much more in an online class than merely moderating online discussions (discussed earlier) or designing the course (see the section on instructional design that follows). Instructors need to provide *clear directions and requirements* for the course (Sheridan & Kelly, 2010), provide *feedback* to students, correct wrong assumptions or faulty perceptions, and also hold students to *high expectations* for learning (Kuh, 2007). Umbach and Wawrzynski (2005) found evidence of greater student engagement when faculty emphasized *higher order cognitive* activities and *challenged* students academically. These acts seem to work for all kinds of students and lead to higher satisfaction with college and higher levels of retention (Kuh, 2007). Xu (2010) tested several ways for the instructor to deliver feedback to students and found that students preferred digital feedback (the instructor used a tablet PC to provide the feedback) and face-to-face conversation. The feedback was credited with increasing engagement, and 80% of subsequent postings to the online discussion were related to feedback on assignments. In fact, research into the role of coaching and feedback (coaching occurred before an online chat and feedback after the chat had occurred) found that they increase higher order thinking over time (Stein, Wanstreet, Slagle, Trinko, & Lutz, 2013). Therefore, providing individualized and detailed feedback to students and doing so in a timely manner are of continuing importance (Sheridan & Kelly, 2010), and such feedback can be offered effectively online.

Feedback to students is also possible through a variety of *student learning assessments*, such as the traditional quizzes, tests, and surveys that online course management systems make possible at regular or random points in the class. Feedback is a hallmark of programmed instruction, where a wrong answer might be both a wake-up call that points out a flaw in students' thinking and a direction to review certain material that has already been covered. Many software systems exist to make the design, delivery, and grading of these assessments either automatic—done entirely by the software—or largely online, leaving the instructor to grade the answers to open-ended questions if that is what he or she chooses to do.

However, an important opportunity exists to use the data generated by online systems (such as course management systems) to help the instructor assess students' learning and engagement in the course. The use of clickstream recording (that captures the record of a student's activity with a technology or especially within a course management system) can help instructors diagnose what the student may be doing incorrectly or not doing at all (Eke, 2008). Other techniques that provide instructors with a profile of what students are doing within their online learning courses are the data on when and how often a student logs into the online class, how much time they are spending on the course's separate sections (such as assignments or units), and their attempts at quizzes. One of the early benefits of tracking student activity online was to identify students who were in danger of dropping out of the class; this has led to more faculty contacting students who have not logged into the class site within the first week of the term to encourage them to engage in the course and to do so before falling too far behind. The effectiveness of such a simple act on the part of the instructor may be due to a perception on the part of the student that the instructor is paying personal attention to him or her, or perhaps the act reminds the student that he or she will be held accountable for learning. Whatever the explanation, students tend to respond with greater engagement in the course.

The data generated by various university data systems have led to the development of the field of learning analytics (Picciano, 2012). *Learning analytics* provides institutional administrators, researchers, and instructors with data on student behavior and learning so that problems at the course, department, and institutional level can be identified, studied in depth, and resolved (Siemens & Long, 2011). Although it may involve collecting new data, most early studies of learning analytics have used existing data (Dziuban, Moskal, Cavanagh, & Watts, 2012). For example, students who log into online courses early and often, participate in discussions and activities, and communicate with instructors are more likely to do well in courses. These activities are similar to those of successful face-to-face students who attend classes regularly, ask questions, and participate in classroom discussions. Also, students with the lowest GPAs perform less well, irrespective of the course delivery method, whether online, blended, or face to face (Dziuban et al., 2012). The role of GPA is not surprising news as it confirms that learners who are struggling academically may be served no better or worse in one delivery mode than another. A good student is a good student irrespective of the medium of learning, and a struggling one will likely struggle in any setting.

Learning analytics can be highly complex (such as social network analysis) or it can be relatively straightforward comparisons of student behaviors (such as time logged into the course). What makes this burgeoning field so interesting is how findings can help instructors identify problem areas or problematic student behaviors and either fix the course design, teach students how to learn online, or improve institutional policy and/or practices. Coates (2006) argues that evidence of how and to what extent students engage with activities that produce learning should appear in quality assurance studies and this is an idea that bears further analysis and possible implementation. Data on student engagement may be hard to define and collect, but perhaps helpful to students and parents evaluating what different colleges or instructional programs offer in the way of appropriate instruction.

Predictive analytics (see http://wcet.wiche.edu/advance/par-framework) uses data from many institutions and provides a unique opportunity to investigate issues across institutions and institutional types, such as identifying predictors of student attrition from online courses. Large data sets are more likely to produce results that can be found across institutional types rather than institution-specific studies that may be identifying idiosyncratic results for one institution or its institutional type, the specific population served by the institution, or its program mix or other factors. In fact, 22 variables discussed in the literature were not predictive of retention, but enrolling in too many courses early in college and taking too many developmental education courses had a negative effect (although having successfully completed those developmental courses had a positive effect), and having a higher GPA, being older in age, and bringing in transfer credits had a positive effect on retention (Sherrill, 2012). For example, students who reenrolled from one term to the next had an average of 36.3 transfer credits versus an average of 11.2 transfer credits for those who did not reenroll, which made the transfer credits the only significant predictor of reenrollment when several demographic variables (e.g., gender, race, age, and a number of institutional variables) were controlled in the analysis (Layne, Boston, & Ice, 2013). Further work will likely enlighten the field of online learning's understanding of what matters and what does not in online student retention and perhaps someday a database of engagement strategies used across programs and institutions may provide detailed analyses of what works across institutions, disciplines, and types of students.

Student Preparation and Skills

Richardson and Newby (2006) also found that engagement improves as students *learn how to learn online.* As students take subsequent online courses, they get comfortable with online technologies and approaches to learning (Song, Singleton, Hill, & Koh, 2004), and they change their learning strategies from more surface strategies to deep strategies or from meeting minimal requirements to intrinsic interest in learning, relating new learning to prior knowledge and connecting ideas across courses and content, and reading materials that go beyond the required texts included on the syllabus. In other words, these students are learning to take responsibility for their learning as they also improve their skills for "learning to learn." Younger students were more likely to use surface strategies; this indicates that instructors teaching primarily traditional-age or undergraduate students should emphasize deep strategies during instructional activities as well as evaluations of assignments.

Engaged students also spend more *time* on their learning (Kuh, 2007) instead of only spending enough time to get by on the assignments. When online students are asked about what helped them learn, time management was a key component for achieving success (Song et al., 2004). And *motivation* also matters (Song et al., 2004); 75% of "A" students in their first year in college say they are highly motivated to succeed, compared to only half of the "C" students (Kuh, 2007). In other words, experiencing success breeds greater motivation for more success, which is as true online as in the face-to-face world.

These findings argue both for assistance to novice online learners and for stressing the importance to students of taking responsibility for their learning and of learning self-regulation behaviors (Sun & Rueda, 2012). Similar problems were noted by Lease (2009), who found that some new students did not "pull their weight" in various group assignments, which created conflict within the group. Such differences among students may argue for using different techniques based on the age or maturity or developmental stage of the student, which needs more attention in the research literature. Such a study was done by Conrad (2002c), who studied students in their first class in an online course; these students were engaged primarily with the course materials (rather than instructors or other students), and instructors were judged on the clarity and completeness of their instructions for assignments. Not surprisingly, student participation in the course, which might result from requirements dictated by the instructor or derive from the students having learned how to learn in the online setting, does lead to greater learning gains (Shin & Chan, 2004). A lack of student participation in a wiki that had been chosen by the instructor to enable collaborative learning highlighted several misconceptions on the part of Cole (2009). Just by using a wiki, the instructor had assumed that students would use it (the "build it and they will come" myth), that students would think that learning how to use the wiki would be a good use of their time, and that all students would find technology "fun." In this situation, participation in the wiki was not required and was termed a failure by the instructor, although the failure may have been due to the instructor making the assignment optional, providing insufficient explanation of the assignment's purpose and importance, and not explaining to students how to develop a wiki for the first time.

Another approach to helping students develop as learners is to support their learning responsible *autonomy*. Stefanou, Perencevich, DiCintio, and Turner (2004) have developed three different approaches that (although developed for the traditional classroom) have obvious applications to the online course. First, instructors can develop students' organizational autonomy by allowing them some decision-making freedom relative to classroom management issues such as with whom to work. Second, they can develop students' procedural autonomy by offering choices to students about which media to use to present ideas. Third, they can develop students' cognitive autonomy by allowing them to evaluate work from a self-referent standard, such as the one that is based on their own professional experiences or prior learning. When an instructor allows students to make some choices that better serve their needs, students develop ownership over the class as well as their learning. In other words, rather than expecting students to have autonomy or learn well in the ways courses are offered, online instructors and designers need to help students move gradually from a novice state (perhaps being a passive learner or unsure of how to learn college material) to a more experienced and mature state (being a responsible, self-disciplined, and proactive learner).

Instructors may also need to express *high expectations* for students. Not only do many students rise to meet these expectations (Reynolds, 1995), but students are clearer about what is required by instructors and what college-level learning entails. Instructors may need to provide greater clarity about what deep learning is and what it looks like and how to do it, which will be a boon to novice and experienced online learners alike.

Although adult learning theory posits that adults prefer to manage their learning so that it can be applicable to their needs, research is needed on how well this works in online learning settings and for whom. Holley and Oliver (2010) found that adult online students increasingly expect to negotiate their use of technology and manage their learning. This finding may indicate two future changes. First, instructors need to clearly identify their students' age, maturity, and willingness to take responsibility for learning and then to design online learning that allows self-management to be learned and rewarded. Second, instructors need to study differences in learning between students who are allowed self-management and those whose learning remains constrained by the design and learning objectives of the course.

Use of Instructional Design

Several researchers have stressed the importance of using instructional design principles during the development of online courses (Fisher, 2010; Meyer, 2002). Online courses can either engage students (or not) based on the pedagogical choices of the course designer, who may be the faculty person in charge of the course or a team of individuals responsible for course development. Clearly, a review of all existing instructional design models is beyond the scope of this monograph, but a review of the earliest and most popular models may be enlightening.

Gagné's (1985) theory of instruction is based on three considerations: learning outcomes (these are in the cognitive, affective, and psychomotor domains), conditions of learning, and nine events of instruction. Although developed prior to the development of online learning, the following nine events can be tied to learning theories and research already reviewed:

1. *Gaining attention.* This involves giving a stimulus to students so that they can pay attention to what follows.
2. *Informing learners of objectives.* The instructor tells students what they will be able to do because of the instruction.
3. *Stimulating recall of prior learning.* The instructor asks for recall of existing relevant knowledge.
4. *Presenting the stimulus.* The instructor emphasizes distinctive features.
5. *Providing learning guidance.* The instructor helps students understand by providing organization and relevance.
6. *Eliciting performance.* The instructor asks to demonstrate learning.
7. *Providing feedback.* The instructor provides feedback on the performance.

8. *Assessing performance.* The instructor requires additional performance and gives feedback to reinforce learning.
9. *Enhancing retention and transfer.* The instructor provides varied practice to generalize the learning.

In a different approach to designing instruction and one that has been applied to online learning, the ADDIE model is an acronym for the five phases described in the model (analysis, design, development, implementation, and evaluation; see Strickland, n.d.). During the analysis phase, the designer specifies the instructional objectives, the learning environment (such as the course management system), and the learners' preexisting knowledge and skills. The model is based on learning theories and explores a variety of pedagogical options as well as software and technology options that have been shown to produce the learning desired. In the design phase, the learning objectives are paired with appropriate student learning assessments, content is designed, lessons planned, and media selected. This phase involves systematic, logical, and orderly development of strategies to produce the desired student learning that involves identifying instructional strategies known to produce specific learning outcomes and developing the visual design of the learning experience. In the development phase, the content, graphics, and technologies are assembled or developed. The implementation phase may involve developing training materials for instructors and learners, if needed, testing to make sure all elements are working, and evaluation of the design. The evaluation phase involves both formative (at appropriate points within the course) and summative (at the close of the course) evaluations, and eliciting both student and instructor comments.

The Systems Approach Model, also known as the Dick and Carey Model (Dick, Carey, & Carey, 2005), has also been used in the development of online courses and has the following steps:

- *Identify instructional goal(s).* Describe a skill, knowledge or attitude that a student will be expected to acquire.
- *Conduct instructional analysis.* Identify what a student must recall and must be able to do.

- *Analyze learners and contexts.* Identify characteristics of the target audience including prior skills, prior experience, and basic demographics and identify characteristics directly related to the skill to be taught.
- *Write performance objectives.* Objectives consist of a description of the behavior, the condition, and criteria (the criteria then become that which judges the student's performance in the evaluation or assessment).
- *Develop assessment instruments.* Involves specific identification of entry behavior needed, pretest, and posttest items.
- *Develop instructional strategy.* Develop preinstructional activities, content presentation, student participation, and assessment.
- Develop and select instructional materials.
- *Design and conduct formative evaluation.* Identify areas of instruction that need improvement.
- *Revise instruction.* Identify poor test items and poor instruction.
- Design and conduct summative evaluation.

This model assumes that the steps are iterated in a parallel and nonlinear fashion, so that what is learned in one step can be immediately applied to others that follow, and later steps may generate a return to earlier steps so that what is learned or decided upon later in the process is incorporated into the course design. The concept of teaching presence likely captures many of these instructional design steps, especially the CoI elements related to the design of the course.

What is perhaps less clear from the language used in these three models is the need for careful scaffolding of learning. This involves first identifying students' current levels of learning, building new learning on prior concepts or theories, and helping students expand or sharpen their thinking. Zhu (1998) found evidence that online discussions could serve this particular purpose so that students could be brought along in their knowledge from basic to ever more complex understanding.

Experienced instructors (be they online or traditional) likely do many of these steps intuitively and without consciously having to go through the entire process. However, understanding instruction as a system that involves such evidently important steps is a worthwhile reminder, especially if the instructor is struggling to understand what may not be working optimally in an online course or if students are struggling with learning what is intended. A return to a systematic approach to course design might remind instructors of any invalid assumptions they have been holding onto, such as that certain pedagogies always work, that they only have a few pedagogies or technologies to choose from, and that students learn in largely similar ways.

What these models, developed often for the pre-Internet world of classroom instruction, do not emphasize are the additional steps needed to deal with choosing the best or optimal medium for the pedagogy chosen. For example, if the pedagogy is discussion, should it be an online asynchronous discussion or a synchronous online chat or live webinar? Is the medium the online discussion board of the institution's course management system (probably the default choice), or a discussion through another system such as Moodle, or Skype, or web-based meeting software (there are several)? The issue then becomes not just what would work well for the learning objectives, but what is available to the instructor and students, what it costs, how much training is involved to use it, and whether technical support is available to help if problems occur.

If the pedagogy chosen involves group work, will it be oriented around solving a problem or producing a project? Will it use wikis or blogs? Wikis allow students to work collaboratively on one product; blogs may also be collaborative efforts, but can also be organized to capture individual contributions. Both are possibly good tools for collaboration, but the software products may present some limitations or affordances. In other words, given the explosion of software products for both wikis and blogs, which one will serve the students' learning needs best? Certainly it ought to be free to use, but how much freedom does it provide students to design their own website and choose a visual appearance they think works best for their purpose? Does it provide a behind-the-scenes discussion space or opportunities for others, such as the instructor, to comment on the wiki or blog? Does it allow for more than one student to be working on the site at the same time? As software programs develop, these elements rapidly change and the instructor needs to be flexible in order to handle new and unforeseen problems. In fact, software programs arise, revise, and are replaced so quickly that it would be impossible to recommend one to use. However, once some of the students are familiar with a few of these programs, they may be relied upon to choose the program that is best for the assignment or that the other students can learn with some assistance from those who have experience with the program or assignment type.

If the student must present his or her work in order to share it with the class, will it be text-based (as in a paper), a PowerPoint presentation (requiring software to capture the slides and audio of the presenter), or multimedia (requiring a certain technical or Internet capacity for each student to create and other students to download)? While posting materials to the Cloud (such as to YouTube or a blog site) gets around the lack of capacity of a course management system, what privacy settings are needed and what understanding of copyright do students need to understand?

Overlaying all of these choices is a concern for engagement of the online student. So, the problem is not simply matching a particular pedagogy with a technology or software, but choosing pedagogies that have been proven to be especially engaging and a technology or software that will work well for the assignment and not present too many problems that can be inherently disengaging. For reasons discussed next, depending on the technology alone to be engaging may be a mistake.

Each of these choices must be based on an understanding of where students are and what they need to learn, what technologies or software programs are available and what their limits are, what pedagogies work and when, and what the course is supposed to accomplish in terms of student learning. The range of decisions to be made is more complex than is usually considered when faculty members design a traditional face-to-face course, and therefore extensive and regular faculty development opportunities are necessary to help them make good decisions.

If the instructor chooses to address student learning styles, what media will be most appropriate for the aural, visual, or kinesthetic learner? Does one provide text and figures (visual), a podcast or audiocast (aural), a physical exercise (kinesthetic), or use multimedia to deliver and assess the learning? Does this choice require special equipment (perhaps a digital recorder for the audiocast) or special permissions (to use copyrighted material)? The next section will take up the challenge of providing multiple paths through the course material in more detail.

Multiple Paths

The interaction of student and activity captures two types of engagement: that of the student with a pedagogy (such as active learning and computer games, interacting in a virtual world, and experiential learning) and personal preferences for engagement of that student. Within this latter category may fall specific activities that are especially engaging to a particular student. For example, the kinesthetic learner may prefer and benefit from learning activities that require more movement such as getting up from the computer and doing something or going somewhere. Other students may prefer to engage in learning that allows them to exercise their artistic sensibilities or logical traits. These preferences may be based on learning styles (e.g., visual, auditory, and kinesthetic), or perhaps Gardner's multiple intelligences, which recognizes a range of cognitive abilities and sensory modalities. Gardner's (1983) multiple intelligences include logical–mathematical, spatial, linguistic, body-kinesthetic, musical, interpersonal, intrapersonal, naturalistic, and existential. These intelligences are not deterministic or exclusive. Individuals often have skills that draw upon more than one intelligence or they develop a new intelligence through life experiences and education. Perhaps the best lesson to keep in mind as one designs online courses is to allow for different modes of learning, if possible, so that students with different strengths can learn more easily but to also provide experience with all types of learning styles or intelligences so that students who can develop alternative or complementary ways of learning are able to do so.

In an evaluation of three online synchronous multiuser environments, greater learning seemed to occur in the situation where students used text chat and two-dimensional still images rather than multiple modes of interaction (MUVEs or Multiple User Virtual Environments) and text-only situations that rely solely on reading (Sullivan et al., 2011). Perhaps not surprisingly, students had more fun in the MUVEs but the simpler approach to interaction (text and two-dimensional images) addressed the needs of student learning styles, whereas the MUVEs appealed to kinesthetic learners (a smaller percentage of students). In any case, perhaps this study also tells us that instructional designs that are highly complex and costly to develop may be less effective in terms of student learning than simpler approaches. Sometimes using simpler photographic images is effective in capturing students' attention and stimulating their thinking (Perry, 2006). However, many more studies that compare ways technology can provide different learning paths for students are needed; furthermore, the assumption that learning styles ought to dictate learning paths should be evaluated given the cost of designing online courses with multiple paths through the content and learning activities.

Use of Technologies and a Caution

After using some form of technology in an online or blended class, many researchers have concluded that the technology affected either student learning or student engagement in learning. For example, Chen and Williams (2009) concluded that multimodel media objects strengthened course interactions and student engagement. Schilling (2009) claimed that use of multimedia applications improved student engagement. Coates (2005) asserted that LMSs (learning management systems or course management systems such as Blackboard or Desire2Learn) could influence student engagement. Burgess (2009) concluded that use of WebCT improved engagement with reading and critical thinking skills of developmental education students.

The question is whether the technology—by itself—had such an effect, which is frankly doubtful. Rather, it may have been technology's novelty that engaged students, the provision of multiple learning paths that support different learning styles, or the different pedagogies made possible with these new technologies or chosen by the instructor to bring about the desired learning. Because many of these studies do not answer these questions, it may be best to consider their findings incomplete until further research can be done. In the past, too many studies of technologies found nonsignificant differences (Russell, 1999) when comparing distance or online courses to traditional or face-to-face courses or found equivocal or uncertain results (these are results that work well in one setting or student type but not in another). Early studies of technology use were not as sophisticated or attentive to the influence of pedagogical choices or instructional design on the appropriateness of technology, which would mean that the technology would be blamed for poor learning like the student complaining about "reading and reading and reading" (Boling et al., 2012, p. 120) online text, which is a clearer criticism of the pedagogy (reliance on passive reading) than the technology chosen. In other words, when researchers attribute student engagement solely to technology, they likely have done an incomplete analysis.

The phenomenon—of attributing effects to the technology—is the result of a number of assumptions that are critically flawed. First, it assumes that technology affects individuals; this may appear to be true, but is over simplified and ignores the greater context, such as the pedagogy chosen for the technology, student skills and preferences, the course objectives, and the range and complexity of influences on individuals separate from technology. Second, it assumes that all students (who have been named the "Net Generation") are equally equipped with technologies and able to use them well. Although many youth are, many others are not. Hughes (2005) noted that some students may have little prior experience with technology due to a range of issues (such as lack of family resources, inadequate instruction in K–12 education, and lack of interest). In contrast to the Net Generation, older generations are characterized as technology-averse, when this is not an accurate description of many older faculty. In both cases, the assumptions are seriously flawed.

However, some researchers do incorporate the pedagogical environment within which the technology was chosen and used. Williams and Chinn (2009) provide an example of using Web 2.0 tools (social networking sites such as Facebook, mash-ups, wikis, and text-based posting such as Twitter) to support experiential learning assignments in a sports promotion course that subsequently led to increased student engagement. Sherer and Shea (2011) also used a Web 2.0 tool—online videos from YouTube—to engage and energize discussions. Lester and Perini (2010) described uses for social networking sites (e.g., Facebook) in the online classroom to engage students in discussions as well as enable group problem solving or projects conducted over the networking site. Junco, Heiberger, and Loken (2010) used Twitter in an experimental group and compared engagement scores using NSSE data to a control group; both groups were involved in collaborative learning projects (i.e., the same pedagogy was used in both settings), but the Twitter users experienced a greater increase in engagement. In all four research studies, the Web 2.0 tools are not credited with having this effect alone; the assignment design made possible by the tools is credited with impacting student engagement. Wankel and Blessinger (2012) have compiled a wide range of technology-based activities (such as wikis, blogs, and webquests) selected to increase student engagement if paired with an intrinsically engaging pedagogy. Another example is the research of Rubin, Fernandes, and Avgerinou (2013) who found that it was not the particular course management system used in online learning, but its "affordances" (p. 48) or the communications and pedagogical options it provides that affected student satisfaction with the course; in other words, it was not the technology, it was what it allowed instructors to do in the course that made the difference to the students. In other words, the distinction between technology as an affordance versus the pedagogy used when using technology ought to be clearly made and appreciated when future studies are analyzed. Technology does not act alone on the student and his or her learning, but it supports and makes possible the pedagogies and activities that are chosen for their ability to bring student engagement and learning about.

Gender, Ethnicity, and Other Differences

So far, research into online learning and student engagement has not found consistent evidence of gender or ethnic differences either in the effectiveness of the engagement practice or effects on learning. Some smaller studies have found slight differences, but the results have been neither consistent across studies nor replicated in multiple studies or a larger study. Either gender or ethnicity does not consistently make a difference on these matters of engagement in online learning, or they do but studies have not found such results. That means better attention needs to be paid to these factors in future studies into online learning in order to resolve this question.

Research using NSSE data suggests that student engagement can and does compensate for many deficits that underserved students may bring to college (Kuh, Cruce, Shoup, Kinzie, & Gonyea, 2008). This is perhaps the best evidence that strong engagement practices, including participating in educational activities that have a clear purpose, can help students earn higher grades and persist in their studies. Although this study was not done on online students, it may provide a hint to what researchers looking into the same issues for online learning may find.

In an extensive treatment of engagement for diverse students in the traditional higher education setting, Harper and Quaye (2009) have stressed the mutual obligation of students to "invest time and effort into academic activities and practices" (p. xxiii) and of institutions to consciously and strategically pursue student engagement. Although weak institutions expect students to engage themselves, institutions that make active use of a variety of student engagement practices may well find that engagement becomes one of several measures of quality for the institution (p. 6). Harper and Quaye (2009) stress the provision of services and/or special engagement practices to better engage a range of student populations, including international students; lesbian, gay, bisexual, transgender, and questioning students; students from minority religious groups; women students in STEM fields; Black male students; part-time, transfer, and returning students; low-income, first-generation students; community college transfer students; and student athletes. Important steps to include are the regular assessment of campus climate, data on student success broken down into subgroups of interest, training for campus constituencies (including faculty, staff, and students from the predominant groups on campus), and proactive advising that reaches out to students and provides assistance or encouragement or a listening ear. This advice may have been developed for the traditional campus, but its advice to address the needs of these special subgroups is relevant for the online classroom as well. The authors conclude that it is important to make the pursuit of student engagement an institutional norm, be it engagement in face-to-face learning or online learning.

Guides to Engagement Online

Three guides to engaging online learners present several activities promoted for their ability to encourage student engagement in the online classroom. Rita-Marie Conrad and J. Ana Donaldson have produced two books: *Engaging the Online Learner* (2011) and *Continuing to Engage the Online Learner* (2012). Activities are categorized into Conrad and Donaldson's four phases of engagement in the first book: newcomer, cooperator, collaborator, and initiator/partner. Each phase calls upon the instructor to perform different roles—social negotiator, structural engineer, facilitator, and community member/challenger—which includes providing activities for students to know each other, to work in dyads to think and reflect, to collaborate in small groups to solve problems, and to contribute to designing their own learning. The first three roles are instructor-centric and the fourth role can be instructor-centric, but it also allows for some leadership on the part of students. In the second volume, Conrad and Donaldson (2012) have five phases of engagement: connect, communicate, collaborate, cofacilitate, and continue. The fifth phase (continue) focuses on the transformation of the learner into a fully functioning, independent, and engaged learner.

The vast majority of the activities in these two books are examples of active learning (such as "Dyad Debate" in Conrad & Donaldson, 2011, p. 72), collaborative learning (such as "Group Wiki" in Conrad & Donaldson, 2012, p. 99), and cognitive engagement (such as "Critical Insight" in Conrad & Donaldson, 2011, p. 86). Readers who need specific tactics for engaging students in online courses are encouraged to review these books for ideas that can be adopted as described or modified to fit the needs of a specific course or discipline. Generally, the tactics seem most appropriate for younger students or students new to online learning (or new to learning to learn), although many activities could be applied to older or more mature students who want to design their own learning. It will be essential that instructors using these activities make it clear to students what the learning objective is; if instructors and designers have learned anything from the research on online discussions, it is that activities need to be chosen for educational reasons.

Barkley (2010) has written *Student Engagement Techniques* that includes 50 "student engagement techniques" that cover eight categories: knowledge, skills, recall, and understanding; analysis and critical thinking; synthesis and creative thinking; problem solving; application and performance; attitudes and values; self-awareness as learners; and learning and study skills. These examples are also heavily oriented to active learning (such as "Seminar," p. 181), collaborative learning (such as "Analytic Teams," p. 207), and cognitive learning (such as "Ethical Dilemmas," p. 313). Many activities are based on collaborative learning, and they go from simple projects to more complex ones (such as "Jigsaw," p. 289).

These engagement techniques are largely based on active and collaborative learning approaches that are considered to be the "hallmark of student engagement" (Lester & Perini, 2010, p. 72). Yet, these techniques can be applied to all kinds of instructional models such as the CoI or the instructional design models discussed earlier. The instructor must choose assignments or activities that will achieve the learning objectives of the course, or make selections of engagement techniques that have a clear and necessary educational objective. Engagement techniques without an educational purpose may be as counterproductive as online discussions conducted without a goal. However, for the instructor who may be stumped on how to engage learners in the content of the online class or the skills they are to learn, Barkley (2010) can provide both specific ideas and activities that can be usefully modified to apply to the course, learning objectives, and student level.

Although all three books are a wealth of activities and ideas for the instructor seeking engagement ideas, course instructors are urged to carefully evaluate their engagement techniques to determine how well they work with their content and students. It is not sufficient to ask whether they worked or not, but professionals in the field of online learning need to also ask why they worked, how well they worked (which may be quantified in some manner), and whether notable exceptions to their effectiveness exist. These evaluations should be prepared for publication and shared in the research literature on online learning and provide new online instructors, and those who are always looking for ways to better their online class experiences, with proven methods for increasing student engagement in online coursework. As higher education is asked to prove its contribution to student learning, it will no longer be sufficient to say that something worked, but to prove it worked.

Research Needed

Despite a long chapter that reviewed many research studies on various tactics purported to increase engagement, many questions remain. So far, many of the studies investigate one method for producing student engagement, and therefore, the field of online learning needs more studies that compare methods of student engagement and clearly specify if differences for various students, learning goals, and disciplines exist. By studying multiple methods at the same time, instructors will gain a sense of which methods may work best in which situations. Hatch (2012) has also argued for instructors and researchers to undertake a more systematic investigation of engagement practices (a) to assess how engagement practices work in combination with other engagement practices or learning theories, (b) to disentangle the various effects of engagement and student characteristics, and (c) to begin triangulation of findings across studies. Hatch (2012) concludes his discussion on student engagement, "we can no longer shy away from the challenge of prying open the black box it remains today" (p. 911). It will take precision in research and repetition of studies across many situations to open the black box of student engagement in online learning.

The field of online instructors and designers also needs to continue to develop a thorough understanding of how to help students who are new to online learning become adept at learning online. Professionals need to better understand if some learning objectives or students exist that are not affected by these techniques. And as instructors undertake their own research into student engagement, they need to pay attention to the context of the learning; this includes more detailed information about student characteristics (not just their age or year in school), learning environments (pedagogies used, technologies or software programs used), and internal environments (such as interpersonal conflicts among students and willingness to help others). The field also needs more studies that provide details about what works and what does not work to engage students online.

Summary

The third chapter provided a detailed overview of research conducted on engagement techniques, from Moore's strategies of student–teacher and student–student, to online discussions, active pedagogies, and instructor actions. It also reviewed research on the role of student preparation and skills on engagement, as well as the role of popular instructional design models and providing multiple paths through the content. However, the fallacy of attributing engagement to technology was cautioned against and differences by gender and ethnicity discussed. Finally, three popular guides to engagement strategies for online learning were profiled, and future research directions were described.

For online instructors and designers, here are some ideas taken from the material discussed earlier:

1. Choose assignments that are active, requiring students to engage in thinking, evaluating, interviewing, discussing, analyzing, creating, comparing, etc.
2. Be clear about the educational purpose of all assignments.
3. Provide clear directions, regular feedback, and set expectations high.
4. Beware of dominating online discussions; know students well enough to adjust your interactions to address their learning needs.
5. Use data available through the course management system to identify students who are struggling, not participating, or not logging in.
6. Design ways that help students learn how to learn; this might include not only general learning skills but also how to learn online.
7. Use an instructional design model when creating new online courses; this helps ensure that courses are comprehensive.

8. Remember that student learning is more likely to be the result of the pedagogy chosen for the assignment rather than the technology.
9. Design courses so that students can pursue different paths through the learning objectives.
10. Get new ideas for engagement techniques by reading good guides that compile project ideas.

Effects From Student Engagement Online

Overview

WITH PRESSURES GROWING ON higher education institutions to enroll and graduate more students, higher education leaders and instructors are looking for ways to improve student retention and graduation rates. Student engagement has been one of several approaches explored for encouraging students to stay enrolled in their coursework through graduation. The next step in this monograph is to ask whether evidence exists that student engagement in online learning has an impact on various outcomes.

The fourth chapter answers the question, "What effects have been found for online student engagement?" It has one purpose: to present and discuss the evidence for the effects of engagement in online learning from the research literature. A certain amount of repetition may be necessary as some of the studies included in prior chapters that focused on the tactics for creating engagement will need to be revisited, but having a separate chapter specific to the evidence for the impact of engagement on other outcomes of interest will help the reader make connections between learning theories and engagement strategies already discussed and the findings specifically for the effects of online engagement. It will also be necessary to extrapolate the mechanism for engagement in several research studies because they were conducted prior to engagement becoming a hot topic for research; this may be a more speculative chapter, but one that is hopefully convincing based on the arguments put forth that connect a study to engagement. (As a reminder of the difference in focus of the third and fourth chapters, Figure 4 captured the fourth chapter's focus on research into the impact of engagement on other outcomes.)

Engagement and Student Learning

In the pre-Internet research on traditional, face-to-face education, the impact of student engagement on student learning was well established (Gellin, 2003; Kuh, Hu, & Vesper, 2000; Pascarella & Terenzini, 1991; Pike & Kuh, 2005). Research conducted in the pre-Internet era is the body of literature that provided a basis for the creation and development of the NSSE research effort and continues to fuel interest in studying aspects of engagement and student learning. This research was instrumental in making the case that student effort had a demonstrated impact on college outcomes (Astin, 1993a; Pascarella & Terenzini, 1991, 2005), including critical thinking and grades although relationships were weak (Carini, Kuh, & Klein, 2006). This last study found that the lowest ability students benefited more from engagement than others. These studies have also confirmed that the time available to the student for study, which is impacted by family and work obligations, also affects how well engagement works to improve student learning. Less time and effort on coursework means less engagement, and therefore, less learning and less progress to graduation. Using NSSE data as well as academic transcripts, merit aid, and ACT/SAT reports, student engagement was also found to have positive, statistically significant effects on grades and persistence between the first and second years of study for students from several racial and ethnic backgrounds (Kuh et al., 2008).

Based on his involvement with the NSSE, Kuh (2008) has recommended that the one thing institutions can do to enhance student engagement and increase student success is to help students participate in at least two high-impact activities, one in the first year and one later in their studies. For first-year students, the activities with proven impact are first-year seminars, learning communities, and service learning. Other proven activities include common intellectual experiences, writing intensive courses, collaborative assignments and projects, undergraduate research, diversity or global learning, community-based learning, internships, and capstone courses or projects. Two comments may be in order to translate Kuh's (2008) recommendations to online learning. First, these activities go well beyond the individual course, which is where much of the prior research into student engagement in online learning has focused. Second, many of these activities can and have been applied to online learning. It may be useful for online programs or online colleges to explore some of these extra-course (or multiple course) engagement practices if increasing student engagement is needed.

As may have become evident in the third chapter, the focus on engagement in online learning tends to center on what is happening with the student in the online course. This may not mean that other influences of engagement are irrelevant (e.g., out-of-class interactions with faculty), but only that many influences become inappropriate or impossible (e.g., involvement in campus groups) because the student is online and living at a distance from campus or working at a full-time job. However, online programs or institutions with many online programs do often provide similar opportunities for their online students; these services can include an online student government organization, extracurricular activities, college sports games televised over the web, and virtual graduation parties.

Qualities of student effort and regulation are one area where engagement has been found to have direct effects on student learning online. As noted earlier, Romero and Barberà (2011) found a correlation of $r = .77$ between number of hours devoted to their classwork and grades, and an even higher correlation of $r = .98$ between hours and time flexibility (number of different times in the day open for classwork). Although the first finding is not surprising—students learn more when they put more time into learning—the second implies that the flexibility afforded to them by online learning has a role in affecting their performance. This reason may be why part-time students and students who are new to online learning (Fisher, 2010) and who face high, initial time commitments and need to learn how to learn online may suffer in their engagement in learning and learning outcomes.

What novice online learners need to learn is how to regulate their learning process and themselves. Self-regulation thoughts and behaviors were significantly correlated with engagement in online courses (Sun & Rueda, 2012);

self-regulation includes regularly logging into (perhaps a simplistic but still valid engagement measure) courses that students report correlates with greater learning or better grades (Davies & Graff, 2005; Shin & Chan, 2004). Students who take more online courses and also take more responsibility for their learning (by adopting deep learning strategies over surface ones) become more cognitively engaged which then correlates with student learning (Richardson & Newby, 2006). Furthermore, students who reached out to others and successfully negotiated group activities experienced various benefits, such as better technology skills and better learning (Askov & Simpson, 2002; Bambara, Harbour, Davies, & Athey, 2009). In other words, participation matters, involvement matters, and participation and involvement affect engagement, which in turn affects student learning.

Instructors who push students to think more deeply about matters, provide clear goals for course activities, or coach students may produce higher order thinking (Meyer, 2004a; Stein et al., 2013; Zhu, 1998, 2006). Instructors who become inappropriately involved with discussions do not. Instructors who choose collaborative learning may find that students are better at synthesizing material and drawing conclusions for their learning (Fu et al., 2009). Active learning produces greater engagement and student learning (Paulus et al., 2006). But instructors should not choose active or collaborative learning solely because it engages; they also need to have a clear educational purpose for its use. If the analogy "interaction for interaction's sake" is applicable to engagement, instructors may need to pursue engagement, not for engagement's sake, but for the sake of student learning. In other words, engagement strategies need to fulfill an education goal that is tied to the course's learning objectives and is communicated to students.

Research based on the CoI has contributed several findings. Teacher presence (especially facilitating discourse) has been found to interact with student interaction and affect online learning effectiveness (Arbaugh, 2005; Arbaugh & Benbunan-Fich, 2006); student engagement in the instructional activities of the course improves learning (Arbaugh, 2000); the teacher's instructional choices can influence students' use of deep approaches to learning and willingness to learn for its own sake (Garrison & Cleveland-Innes, 2005); the instructor's careful use of questions and guidance can produce higher levels of critical discourse in the course (Garrison & Cleveland-Innes, 2005); and use of the CoI to guide course redesign improves student learning outcomes (Swan et al., 2012).

One criticism of the research on the CoI and student learning is the lack of a robust assessment of learning (Rourke & Kanuka, 2009). Even when an item in a study refers to student learning, it often captures only students' perception of their learning or assesses their perception of how much was learned. Without a better measurement of student learning, one that is objective and more complex than indicating that "I learned a lot in this course," research on the effects of the CoI on student learning is hampered. Practitioners of online teaching need to know how best to produce the learning intended, and although the CoI model provides a well-rounded and justified approach to online course design, the practitioner may still not know how to produce learning specific to his or her course and discipline. Not surprisingly, more research is needed to provide more granular information about what specifically works for specific students in specific learning environments.

Engagement and Other Outcomes

Engagement in course activities produces greater *student satisfaction* with the course (Shin & Chan, 2004; Swan, 2001), and social presence (a gauge of the individual's engagement with others in the course) has a positive correlation with student satisfaction with e-learning as well (Arbaugh & Benbunan-Fich, 2006). Efforts to engage learners online have also been found to produce a greater sense of *community* within the course (Conrad, 2002a; Robinson, 2010) and increased *retention* within a learning program (Meyer et al., 2006; Shin & Chan, 2004). In fact, when courses were redesigned using the CoI, Vaughan (2010) found that the student retention rate climbed to 100%.

In other words, instructors who make an effort to engage their online learners by making wise choices in assignments and their own activities in the course can make a difference for students. However, instructors need more help making the right choice for the learning needed and the students enrolled. In other words, the devil is in the details.

Research Needed

Because the focus in the research on engagement has been the online course, online learning instructors and designers do not know the effect of the other services mentioned earlier (virtual student government; web telecasts of graduation ceremonies or sports games) on student engagement in online programs. Faculty especially need to undertake research into these out-of-class influences on online students to confirm whether or not, or to what extent, these influences impact student learning, retention, and satisfaction with their online education.

Research is also needed to focus on the extent to which engagement tactics affect other outcomes of interest, including student learning but also retention in the program, achievement of online community, and satisfaction with online coursework. It is not sufficient to rely on the research conducted in the pre-Internet era to claim that pursuing student engagement has an effect on positive outcomes of interest to institutions and students; instructors and designers involved in online learning must prove such an effect for online learning specifically. Although it is unfortunate that online learning has to continue to prove itself to students and the public, those who teach online or manage online programs must continue to pursue such proof. The credibility of what instructors do online depends upon continued research into the impact on learning of engagement strategies in the online setting, the extent to which they impact outcomes of interest, for whom they work, where in the curriculum they work, and why they work. As many online instructors who can do so should embrace this obligation with enthusiasm.

Summary

The focus of this chapter is a review of the research related to the effects of ensuring student engagement in online courses. Based in part on research on engagement in pre-Internet as well as online coursework, engaged students have improved learning as captured by grades or test scores. Evidence also exists for the importance of student effort and regulation on learning, which engagement may influence. Also, research on retention in online courses found improvement with increased student engagement, improving to 100% retention in some special circumstances.

The material in the fourth chapter leads to the following insights:

1. Engagement activities likely influence the amount and level of student learning, including the student's higher order thinking.
2. Engagement also seems to produce higher student satisfaction as well as retention rates.
3. The impact of engagement activities (both singly and in combination) needs to be studied further.

Limits to Student Engagement

Overview

ADVOCATES FOR AN INNOVATION or a practice often find themselves lobbying others as if their innovation could solve all problems. But that is rarely the case. Students are complex and have many aspects to their personalities and influences upon them that could prevent engagement strategies from working as wished.

This chapter asks this critical question, "Are there limits to student engagement?" The intent is not to encourage professionals in online learning to throw up their hands in despair and avoid efforts at engaging all students. However, professionals may need to understand their failures and undertake further study of what may work with such students, if not now, then at some later point in time. This chapter will review research that addresses personal, social, or other limits to engagement. These may include personal qualities (discipline or drive) and time limits (resulting from family demands or employment obligations) as well as limits of instructional expertise. To the extent possible, the review will recognize situations where student engagement may not be likely to result from various engagement activities and will eschew blanket generalizations in favor of specific, research-based insights and exceptions to those lessons.

Characteristics of Students

Several student characteristics have been found to impinge on the student's ability to engage in learning. For example, *student effort* has a demonstrated impact on college outcomes (Astin, 1993a; Pascarella & Terenzini, 1991,

2005). Therefore, influences that might impact that effort would be significant barriers to student learning and other outcomes of interest (e.g., retention and graduation). For example, *part-time status* of the student is related to engagement in online courses (Fisher, 2010) due in part to the student being less committed to earning a degree or having other demands on his or her time. *Time limitations* due to a student's professional and family obligations plague not just the adult working professional, but the traditional-age student who must work either part time or full time to support his or her college attendance. Romero and Barberà (2011) discussed how to make *time-on-task* within an online course be more quality time-on-task, which recognizes both the importance of having time for learning but also the importance of flexible time commitments for working students (e.g., mornings are best for these students). Another influence of time is the *expansion of time available* that occurs because online students have more time flexibility to participate in online discussions since they are not limited to participating only during course schedules, such as 10 a.m. to noon on Tuesdays and Thursdays, as is common in traditional on-campus schedules (Harasim, 1990). Romero and Barberà (2011) also emphasize the quality of *cognitive time* (rather than solely the quantity of time spent on learning), which can include focus, information-processing capacity, consciousness, and higher order cognitive skills as in decision making (p. 126). *Proactive behavior* (such as organizational actions taken by the student in advance of a situation) has also been found to affect student engagement levels, especially for women (Peters et al., 2011). And evidence is growing that *prior experience with online learning* encourages greater student engagement (Fisher, 2010); this finding implies that first-time students who are new to college study or online coursework may be especially prone to a lack of engagement. Therefore, specifically addressing these students' online skills, fears, and understanding of how to learn online may be extremely helpful.

Three other characteristics of first-time students may also be problematic to learning online. First of these is a *lack of experience with constructivist* methodologies and a preference for traditional pedagogies; such students are comfortable with teacher-centered pedagogies and may feel uncomfortable being asked to learn differently. The second characteristic is related to the first: less experienced and/or successful students may need help *learning self-regulatory behaviors* that include learning how to learn, increasing one's motivation, and planning and evaluating one's learning (Boekaerts, 2011). Boekaerts (2011) argues that self-regulation behaviors need to be learned and scaffolded (much as content knowledge also needs to be scaffolded) with the assistance of another person (instructor or more advanced peer) who can provide "next steps" for the learner. In a critique of a virtual community building project, Pyrtle, Powell, and Williamson-Whitney (2007) found that greater attention needed to be paid to developing student motivation; without it, the task of building and maintaining a useful community was difficult to achieve. Learners without these skills and sufficient motivation are at a disadvantage, although these skills can be nurtured or taught. A third characteristic is a *preference for face-to-face* instruction (Fisher, 2010), which may have been the only instructional model experienced in high school or earlier college courses. Certainly, some individuals do prefer such contact, but what portion of those who say this do so because they think instruction occurs (or should only occur) in this format? This argues for colleges to take a more proactive approach to weaning students from prior instructional models, addressing preconceptions about what teaching and learning are, and explaining how and why the pedagogies of online learning may work better for them and how they may learn more with these approaches.

In a similar vein, Taplin (2000) and Hoffman and Ritchie (1997) have found that some students have *trouble changing their dependent or passive learning habits* after many years of teacher-centered instruction. They may feel discomfort when asked to be more independent, resist changes, and blame the teacher for not having taught them as they are accustomed. Hadwin and Oshige (2011) proposed that student engagement is the result of students' motivation and goals for learning, which means that students having serious problems with identifying or developing *self-motivation or goals* for their learning may be at a severe disadvantage. Layne et al. (2013) hypothesized that students' personal characteristics such as an inability *to delay gratification* or *impaired self-efficacy and resilience* influence the student's ability to persist in their education. These qualities in students may need to be proactively addressed by institutions, including developing a student's comfort with active learning, motivation, and goal setting, as well as self-efficacy and resilience.

The student's perception of the relevance of the learning opportunities offered may also need to be directly addressed by instructors. This is because engagement is the result of the students' "perceived relevance of the learning situation, relevant self-perceptions, and perceived action possibilities for engagement" (Boekaerts, 2011, para. 5). McCaslin and Burross (2011) found that students who *do not see themselves as learners* may be more difficult to engage. These findings provide a clue to not only which students may be difficult to engage, but also why. In other words, learners possess beliefs, values, and abilities that affect their motivation, willingness to learn, and engagement in learning. This may explain why so many instructors remark upon the psychological and learning-related neediness of some students. The causes may be any of the above qualities—lack of goals, preference for passive learning, or a lack of learning skills—but high-maintenance (or stated in a more colloquial manner, "needy") students tend to require continual reassurance that they are doing the assignment correctly and they require more, and more detailed, instructions from the instructor. The issue here is the excessiveness of the requests, because all students ask questions and require some positive feedback. High-maintenance students may not have read the assignment instructions and prefer the instructor to tell them what to do in a one-to-one setting. This of course takes instructor's time and does not develop the student as a more self-reliant learner.

These issues may play a role in students' lack of participation in online courses. It is not clear from the research why "lurkers" (students who read online discussions or blog posts but do not post their own thoughts online) and lurking happen. These students may be *hesitant or unwilling* to post their thoughts, being more insecure or less confident in their ability to contribute something of value (Gilbert, Morton, & Rowley, 2007). These problems may be why so many instructors require participation in discussions and offer points for student participation in online discussions based on the number of postings or the quality or depth of those postings. Research conducted so far does not yet explain the motivations of lurkers and all of their reasons for lurking, which means that instructors' understanding of student behavior online remains incomplete and possibly faulty (Preece, Nonnecke, & Andrews, 2004).

Although developed for traditional instruction, work on student typologies may have some usefulness for understanding the persistence of online students. Hu and McCormick (2012) studied student typologies and found different persistence rates by type of student. Maximizers, conventionals, unconventionals, academics, and collegiates had persistence rates over 90%, and the disengaged and grinds had persistence rates of 87.8%. Other typologies have been proposed by Astin (1993b) and Kuh et al. (2000), who identified different student types, but also different outcomes for the different types. Given the lack of consistent findings of student types, perhaps this is an area for future research into the role of student engagement in online learning.

What is important to remember is that none of these characteristics mentioned earlier—part-time attendance, having work obligations, or a lack of experience with online learning—dictate failure or preclude a student from learning successfully in the online course. In fact, ample examples exist from many campuses that such students do overcome their time limitations or lack of experience or poor self-confidence and persist to graduation. What these characteristics do indicate is that whenever institutions, instructors, or staff encounter students with these characteristics, additional assistance is needed, be that more encouragement, early intervention, opportunities to develop skills and attitudes, or proactive advising.

Characteristics of Instruction

Furthermore, poor instruction (this is to be construed as both instructional deficiencies in the design of the course and the daily oversight of the online course) plays an important role in eliciting or failing to elicit student engagement (Mason, 2011). In a survey of online students, *course design* received the most mentions as both a positive and a negative contributor to student satisfaction with online learning (Song et al., 2004). These results explain why early online courses that heavily depended on reading text often experienced higher student attrition. Given the importance of student engagement in "educationally purposeful" (Hu & McCormick, 2012, p. 739) activities, course activities that are done for other purposes may not always be helpful for student engagement or learning. For example, providing opportunities to socialize in an online course (such as to share developments in students' lives) may certainly contribute to a sense of community or of knowing one's peers, but for some students it may not be a good educational use of their time, especially if their time is at a premium due to other demands. Early in the development of online education, emphasis on *interaction for interaction's sake* (see the fourth chapter) in online coursework may have been problematic, pursued because interaction was thought to be worthwhile or an important avenue for learning to occur. However, given the current understanding of the importance of pursuing educationally relevant activities, interaction needs a purpose or goal. Wilson (2004) and Meyer (2005) shall stand in for many early research studies that focused on student interaction that did not have a clear educational purpose or charge to the group undertaking the online discussion. Or as Garrison and Cleveland-Innes (2005) concluded after a review of the literature, "interaction is not enough" (p. 133). Zhu (2006) added that interaction is not always beneficial to the instructional process.

Poorly designed online courses may be a large contributor to poor student engagement. As noted earlier, these may include activities that are chosen by the instructor because they *validate the faculty person's ego* or are consistent with his or her conceptions of the appropriate role of an instructor (Rose, 2012). Rose also mentions the importance of faculty accepting their loss of complete control over the educational process and willingness to respond to student emails throughout the day (and possibly night). These insights imply that sometimes the design of the course has more to do with the psychological or emotional needs of the instructor and his or her preconceptions about how learning happens. In fact, online learning may have had a role in encouraging the movement away from teacher-centric discourse (Anderson, 2008) and toward learning- or student-centered discourse, although this proposition still needs to be confirmed by more research. Arbaugh (2000) also found that improving the *instructor's online pedagogical skills* impacts the online learning experience of students in a marked fashion. This may be due simply to the lack of preparation of many faculty in methods of teaching (whether face-to-face or online), a lack of information about the relative impact on student learning of various pedagogical choices, or a lack of understanding of the range of technologies or software products available to them. However, when asked, some students do not place much importance on face-to-face or synchronous communications (Sheridan & Kelly, 2010), which may help faculty let go of personal and professional beliefs and values that have stressed the importance of synchronicity and the face-to-face interaction.

Another set of problems can be attributed to attempting to provide the face-to-face classroom experience within the online class. McBrien, Jones, and Cheng (2009) adopted the use of synchronous software to fill this perceived void and found that online chats were dominated by some students (one suspects they may have typed the fastest), were unable to maintain a sequence of questions and answers that caused confusion, and were inconvenient to some of the students. Synchronicity tended to create more difficulties than it solved and thus did not contribute to student engagement or learning.

Poorly designed online discussions are also problematic not only because they have unclear or diffuse educational objectives, but instructors may provide poor or inadequate instructions to students or they may dominate the discussion and thereby defeat the educational purpose of discussing material online. As Zhu (2006) concludes, "it is unrealistic to assume that online discussions will engage and improve interaction between students and instructors and among students themselves under any circumstances" (p. 470). In fact, "knowledge construction did not come naturally to the online discussion" (p. 471). Examples of these problems follow.

Evidence for the impact of *poor or unclear expectations* is common in the literature. Coole and Watts (2009), despite offering an extensive website and discussion board, found that students did not personally engage in these but limited their involvement to reading others' posts or asking questions; this may be due to the instructor not providing *sufficient clarity on what they expected* students to do on the discussion board and reasons why they should participate, or it may be due to a lack of incentive to participate. The opposite may also be true; too much participation in online discussions can be a problem. Kay (2006) found that having *too many discussion entries* to read could actually decrease student participation and create a situation where later entries were not read by all students.

Online instructors or designers often provide *poor or unclear directions* to students about the purpose of online discussions; poor directions led to students mostly sharing their personal experiences rather than engaging in evidence-based reasoning (Angeli, Valanides, & Bonk, 2003). Mason (2011) found that despite using real-life problems and a discussion forum for online coursework, the students did not engage in these tasks because the instructor had not adequately explained the task and the reasons for participating and was not proactive in moderating the discussion. Both Gilmore and Warren (2007) and Dykman and Davis (2008) stressed the need for faculty to interact and reinforce learning in the online classroom.

However, can *faculty play a too dominant role* in discussions? How are they to participate in online discussions? The answer may depend on the type of student and the goal of the discussion. For some younger or more naïve students, instructors may need to provide encouragement or provide a clear focus on the task at hand in the online discussion. However, for some of these students, instructor pronouncements in an online discussion are treated as correct and discussion ends; such students may need instructor approval to feel they are discussing correctly or providing the "right answers." For fields where finding right answers are important, this seems reasonable, but for fields where the student should be learning to reason and to do so independently, the task is for instructors to move dependent students to more independent thinking. For older and more experienced students, instructors may participate as equals, offer occasional encouragement, or withhold comment to encourage better discussions. For discussions that do not have a clear purpose, instructors may need to intrude to give them direction, which is why online discussions need a goal best provided by the instructor or student discussion leader at the moment the discussion begins or preferably during the design of the course. When instructors are absent in the discussions, they may convey a lack of interest in students; when instructors respond to every message, the discussion may become stifled (Zhu, 2006). This represents a tricky balance between recognizing contributions and keeping a hands-off stance toward the discussion. As Shea et al. (2010) also noted, sometimes instructors who post a lot take over the discussion, when posting less and making one's posts more targeted to student learning are more effective. The issue of how and when instructors participate in online discussions does not have one clear, consistent answer.

Arbaugh (2010) clarifies some of these concerns about *instructor activity*. Using the CoI model, he found that both the teaching presence and immediacy behaviors (those behaviors that reduce social and psychological distance) of the instructor were positive predictors of student perceived learning and satisfaction with online learning. But here is what is interesting: instructor login intensity (the average amount of time spent per login) was a negative predictor of student learning. This may capture the faculty's inappropriate or excessive effort to impact the course activities or discussions, which may be intrusive, confusing, or demotivating to students. In other words, too much instructor input may be less helpful to student learning than the instructor's focused, learning-related input. Zhu (2006) concludes that an instructor's overinvolvement or inappropriate involvement in online discussions may also negatively impact student cognitive engagement in the discussion. In other words, the best influence faculty may have on learning is through design of the instructional experience before the semester begins and thoughtful moderation of the discussion as it occurs.

As noted earlier, attention placed on the *needs of instructors* as they move to online teaching is not misplaced. Shea, Pickett, and Li (2005) found four factors to be significantly associated with faculty satisfaction with online learning: level of interaction with their online course, technical support, a positive experience while developing and teaching the course, and the perceived appropriateness of online learning for the discipline (math/science, humanities, and business/professional faculty tend to express higher levels of satisfaction with online delivery). Instructors who are not developed and supported for online teaching may be poorly prepared for the transition to online, design online courses that do not support student learning, and do a less-than-excellent job in the course, which would affect student experiences during the course. Faculty need ample instructor development, but also ongoing support. For example, Schulte, Dennis, Eskey, Taylor, and Zeng (2012) described the effects of providing new online instructors with immediate evaluation and mentoring as they teach their courses rather than waiting for an end-of-course student evaluation to identify problem areas.

Fortunately, several tools to improving course design are available, including use of the Quality Matters rubric (see https://www.qualitymatters.org/) or the CoI model or many others. Research on use of the CoI to guide course redesign by deliberately attending to concepts captured by items included in the instrument found an improvement in student learning outcomes (Swan et al., 2012) as well as greater student engagement (Vaughan, 2010). Other policies, including faculty development for online teaching and policies requiring or rewarding improvement of faculty online teaching skills, may also be important ways of eliminating poor instruction. In addition, a range of teaching skills (high expectations, quick feedback) may be just as applicable and important to online teaching as the face-to-face methods and philosophies that preceded them. In other words, good teaching is good teaching (Ragan, 1999) wherever it occurs and includes several skills that are the same or similar in both settings. Certainly, online learning may require certain new skills (e.g., manipulating technologies), but many skills are no different from the face-to-face setting. For example, teachers in both settings need to identify needed content, design approaches for students to learn the content, and evaluate student learning. Working within an LMS (learning management system such as Blackboard or Desire2Learn) to communicate with students and host online discussions, assigning the development of a wiki as a way to encourage collaborative work, or meeting with students over Skype to advise and/or answer student questions requires some knowledge and skill with manipulating current software packages, but each also depends upon selecting a pedagogy that meets the learning needs of the student.

Clark-Ibáñez and Scott (2008) shall perhaps stand in for many articles that chronicle the transformation of face-to-face instructors to online instructors; suggestions include ways instructors can prepare students to learn online, encourage learning through online discussions, incorporate multimedia, and evaluate the course and student learning. In other words, these are the skills of the traditional instructor, which have been modified somewhat to include early planning, purposeful choices to engage students, and understanding how to use various technologies to ensure student learning. Meyer (2004b) once conceptualized the explosion of comparison studies in the literature, which compared the outcomes of a course offered through traditional methods versus a course offered through distance education, as a way that individual instructors document their journey from one mode of instruction to another. These kinds of studies can be thought of as "personal journey research," and although they may not contribute the kind of valid and reliable research results needed, they do capture how an individual comes to better understand teaching in the new medium.

Research Needed

This chapter has identified reasonable limits to the effectiveness of adopting engagement strategies due to various student characteristics. However, these limits need to be understood in more detail. Is it true that all students may not be affected by engagement strategies? Will a focus on engagement, for example, not yield 100% student retention or even near-perfect learning? If not, who will be affected, when is engagement most fruitfully applied, and what theory explains why the engagement strategy worked (or not) with a particular student or group of students? For a student facing a limiting condition such as inexperience with online learning or multiple time demands, how much can engagement strategies overcome? Does it matter who provides the engagement strategy—staff or instructor, family member or friend? These questions, when answered, can help instructors and institutions that serve students who might have problems with engagement to develop better engagement approaches that are supported by research; ultimately, the goal is to more effectively engage those students who can be engaged.

Characteristics of instruction also contribute to failures of engagement. Research is needed on how much (and for which students) engagement increases as instruction moves to educationally purposeful activities, clearer guidance on what students need to do and achieve, and active or collaborative learning principles. Instructors also need to better understand what level of involvement in a class is appropriate, especially in online discussions, given different learning objectives, disciplines, and maturity levels of the students. Certainly, research on faculty development efforts is needed to document the effects of training on the course design of online courses and student outcomes (including engagement, but also student learning and retention).

The sixth chapter summarizes the findings from this review of the current research literature and extends the lessons so that students of engagement may test the lessons and expand upon them with their own studies into student engagement in online learning.

Summary

This chapter included a lengthy discussion of the limits to engagement as drawn from the research and theoretical literature. In other words, characteristics and behaviors of students as well as of instructors can limit the level of engagement online students can reach. Becoming aware of and addressing these characteristics and behaviors may help improve student engagement in the future.

Online instructors and designers may need to keep in mind that students may limit the effectiveness of engagement strategies. Students may:

1. provide poor effort, be attending part-time, or have insufficient time available to do the coursework;
2. be less likely to be proactive in their learning, to possess motivation to overcome obstacles, or to self-regulate their own behavior to ensure success, or simply not know what it takes to learn;
3. not have any prior online learning experience and be unsure of what to do; and
4. not like or be unexperienced with constructivist pedagogies or prefer face-to-face learning and passive learning approaches.

But online instructors and designers may especially need to pay attention to the limits of instruction:

1. Poor course design is the culprit in many bad online courses.
2. Interaction done for interaction's sake and without clear, educational objectives does not lead to learning.

3. An instructor's inappropriate domination of online class activities, especially discussions, may harm student learning.
4. The instructor's poor online pedagogical skills may lead to passive instruction and poor student engagement.

Next Steps

Overview

HIGHER EDUCATION LEADERS need to know what they can expect from efforts to increase online programs as well as engagement strategies in online courses. Online instructors and designers need to know what works in their efforts to engage online learners. And everyone needs to know what questions remain so that answers can be pursued. In other words, what are our next steps in the pursuit of student engagement in online learning?

This chapter answers the question, "What can be concluded about how to increase student engagement in online learning?" It will draw on the major themes within the prior chapters, including identifying useful theories for increasing online student engagement and making some recommendations to guide efforts at increasing student engagement in online coursework, to guide future research studies into online learning and engagement, and to provide helpful directions to online educators. It will first address the interests of online instructors and designers and then those of higher education administrators.

Theories to Use

The review of the literature has resulted in some clear directions to online instructors and designers about theories that can be useful in the design and operation of online courses. *Active learning* challenges the student to get personally involved in his or her learning and to act, decide, create, and evaluate their own learning project or product. This is one powerful definition of engaged learning. It replaces passivity with personal involvement and directs instructors to avoid passive learning options (such as the lengthy lecture or reading assignment) with directions for the student to do something to produce, test, or apply his or her learning. Active learning does not mean the end to lecturing or reading, but once instructors understand its effectiveness, they will design activities that push students to take course material and apply it, expand upon it, connect it to solving problems, understand the implications of the content more deeply, find fault with it (just because content is spoken by a professor or published in textbooks does not mean it is always correct), and create new content. In other words, strategies that are based on active learning will most likely be engaging to students.

Collaborative learning is another learning theory that the research indicates is possibly engaging. It involves the student actively interacting with others to an educational purpose, coordinating the group's initial analysis of the problem, developing a means for tackling the problem's study and resolution, and negotiating the group's final understanding that results from its discussions. This involves a give-and-take among group members, identifying areas of agreement and disagreement, designing and undertaking a process for resolving disagreements, using data or other authorities (e.g., major authors or theories) to resolve disputes, and crafting a common answer with appropriate identification of the pros and cons of various solutions. And all of this is done by negotiating among contrasting personalities, individuals with a variety of interests, and students who possess a range of strengths and weaknesses. Asking for collaboration seems to be a deeply engaging task for most students.

The *CoI model* (as well as the other instructional design models described earlier) is a framework for designing online courses that pays attention to the elements (social presence, teaching presence, and cognitive presence) that combine to make a worthwhile learning experience. The CoI model can be beneficially combined with active and collaborative learning as the instructor chooses educational activities that can be engaging for the students involved in the online course. When the CoI model is guiding the design and instruction of an online course, it helps to address what students are asked to do, how and why they are to do it, and what the instructor is doing and to what purpose.

Instructor, Know Your Students

However, and this is an important caveat, not all students respond equally well to active learning or collaborative learning (or any specific kind of learning). Online instructors and designers cannot assume that any theory or strategy is a guaranteed way to increasing engagement; it may be a fallacy because some students may learn best reading and thinking by themselves and may respond poorly to instruction designed to be incessantly active or collaborative. And for some groups of students (especially those with jobs and families), the time needed to work in groups may be difficult to find and can become a barrier to their participation in online coursework. Students are different from each other and even from themselves at different times or in different contexts. Engagement is an individual process that awakens interest in learning and stirs the motivation to learn.

Faculty members need to know their students as they are and not as faculty would wish them to be or think they ought to be. Faculty may need to discard prior perceptions of the "traditional student" that existed in the past or for a particular institutional type. In other words, faculty may need help from institutional researchers and others who study the current group of enrolled students to be able to grasp the realities of current students, such as how many work part or full time, what percentage may learn best actively, which learning pedagogies work best for most students, and what kinds of students need what kinds of help.

Quite simply, online instructors and designers need to know how their students learn best and when to modify pedagogical strategies for a reasonable exception for a particular student or type of student. Perhaps the best advice for instructors and designers is to offer options in tackling educational projects so that students can choose the learning option that fits their preferences or needs best. Or the course can include a variety of engagement tactics, some of which will work for some students some of the time and others that will work with other students at other times. Striving for a variety of options is likely a good, basic strategy for any online course, although pairing strategies to specific students is ideal. Or, when the educational objectives require a particular approach, students may need to be provided with a rationale for why that pedagogical approach is the best one for student learning and/or the objectives of the course or degree program.

The one important conclusion is that online instructors and designers need to keep exploring engagement strategies and when they work and for whom. Certainly, online instructors and designers may not always be successful in this hunt for the best engagement strategy or even the best strategy for now; the important lesson is to keep exploring the nexus of student needs, differences, and what works to keep them engaged in their online courses.

Learn How to Learn

Perhaps before students can become engaged in their online coursework, they may need help from online instructors and designers on how to improve their own learning skills. Students often need to develop their capacity for self-discipline or self-regulatory behaviors, for knowing how to motivate themselves, for setting goals and delaying gratification, and for developing attitudes or behaviors that are critical for learning. They need help learning what to pay attention to, how to study, and where to find answers to their questions. They need to learn how to learn new ideas and concepts, the role of scaffolding, repetition, and focused attention. They must learn how much effort learning will take, but that it becomes easier with practice and dedication, and finally, that learning has its personal and professional rewards.

To assume that students always arrive with these attitudes and skills will likely continue to prove problematic for colleges and especially for online programs. And to assume that these skills are deficient only in students who are new to college or have less-than-stellar high school records is to miss the relatively good and willing students who may need assistance learning how best to learn online. It will be increasingly problematic for online programs to assume that students have the skills they need to succeed or to assume that telling them they need discipline will develop that attitude. Online educators may need to purposefully design early learning experiences that develop these important attitudinal and intellectual skills.

Of course, students have an obligation to develop themselves into the kinds of learners who can succeed in various learning environments. They may need first to realize they have a deficiency and how they can work on developing these attitudes and skills.

Be Clear About Educational Objectives

Although online instructors and designers have willingly adopted a variety of pedagogical approaches (online discussions, for one), they have often been unclear about the educational purpose of these pedagogies. If some approach has been touted in the literature as good for online learning, it was tried. But much like learning in the face-to-face classroom, online courses may have been unclear about the purpose or educational objectives of the exercise. Instructors and designers may have assumed that if they do the right things in the class, then the right learning would result. The process would work, like magic. But research tells us that if online courses do not provide purposeful and clear objectives and details about what students are to learn, how they are to proceed, and what criteria will be used to evaluate them, student learning may be a "hit-or-miss" affair. Online instructors and designers need to be clear with students, explain about the process to be used, why it has been chosen, and what steps they should take. One need not subscribe to the four-stage cognitive presence process of the CoI, because many other problem-solving approaches do exist, but choose one that fits the educational objectives or the culture of the discipline. Or develop a rubric for course assignments or online discussions or search for one online and share with students so they know what they need to do. But at minimum be clear about what the objectives for an activity are and the steps that must be taken to achieve them.

Some Lessons About Engagement Strategies

First, engagement is not always possible in all instructional situations and for all students. Sometimes learning requires difficult work that is not immediately attractive or engaging to a particular student. And sometimes students face too many barriers to overcome. However, although there may be a limit to what can be achieved by using engagement strategies online, it is not clear at the current moment what that limit may be. So it is important for instructors and designers to keep trying and studying what works, but recognize some mountains may be difficult (although never impossible) to scale.

Second, even the short review above of strategies that increase student engagement in online courses supports the conclusion that engagement strategies for online learning may be the same, or nearly the same, as strategies for face-to-face classes. Providing immediate feedback works, student–faculty interaction works, and assessing student learning works, but these work well irrespective of the learning setting. That means as research on engagement in face-to-face settings is published, online instructors and designers may use the strategies with some confidence that they will work in online courses as well.

That means the search for engagement strategies should not be limited solely to books or articles or studies about engagement in online learning, but can include engagement strategies found to work in traditional classrooms. In other words, what works to increase student engagement in the face-to-face classroom will most likely increase student engagement in online learning. A corollary of this finding is that an online equivalent exists to face-to-face tactics for increasing student engagement. Modifications to the engagement strategy may need to be made, but most modifications will pertain to the technology or software used, not the strategy. For example, active learning may be conducted within a face-to-face class and involve group projects, but active learning online may need an online space (such as a discussion board) or a web-based conversation for organizing, discussing ideas, and planning the group's efforts. In other cases, little modification may be needed; experiential learning may require a student participate in a group or activity outside of class, but this is true for experiential learning that occurs in both face-to-face and online courses. In other words, the literature on student engagement in the pre-Internet world may be very useful for online educators. Furthermore, as online engagement strategies are proven to work, they may have an application to the more traditional classroom. Engagement may be engagement wherever it occurs.

Third, although early retention theories (Tinto, 1998) and the NSSE stressed the role of out-of-class campus clubs and social opportunities (e.g., athletic games, service clubs) in student engagement with the campus or college, online courses and programs may have to depend more heavily on in-class activities to increase student engagement. In other words, achieving student engagement in the online class may be even more critical to keeping students enrolled and progressing through their academic program. However, several institutions with large online student enrollments have opted to offer virtual student governments or other innovations to better tie students to the institution.

Fourth, because the needs of online students vary, it is important to understand how different groups may feel differently about a type of engagement strategy. For example, adult working professionals may have less interest or time for participating in student groups, and less need for socializing in a class because their social needs are met through their jobs, families, and circle of friends. No one strategy can work for all students and all courses.

Instructor, Know Yourself

Instructors are individuals with beliefs about the world, how learning happens, and how they ought to perform in their professional positions. As noted earlier, they may have expectations about what a college student should be able to do, how students learn, and what their job is. Unfortunately, these beliefs are sometimes based on inaccurate assumptions. As the earlier section on recognizing that not all college students know how to learn may attest, students have been changing and so has the job of the faculty person or instructor. Some instructors may hold the expectation that the students have the responsibility to adjust to the demands of college, to learn as they are taught, and to produce the learning outcomes expected. Such instructors believe that their job is to teach and the students' job is to learn. Some of these instructors may have a view of their professional role as the deliverer of content (which perhaps explains the continued reliance on lecture and instructor-centric approaches) rather than as the person who challenges, critiques, supports, and creates learning situations. Their egos may be inordinately tied to being the center of the class or having their needs or desires dictate the course's design, which leads them to dominate online discussions rather than focusing on the needs of students. To these instructors, engagement strategies may appear to be an inappropriate catering to students whose job is to be engaged in what is taught. Obviously, these attitudes on the part of the instructor may be responsible for designing an online course that is less than successful in terms of student learning.

It is important that higher education values, supports, and rewards instructor renewal that specifically addresses changing conceptions of what an instructor is or does. Instructors also need to feel an obligation to reevaluate their beliefs and expectations regularly in light of changing student needs and realities. The fault may lie in old or outmoded personal or professional beliefs, rather than always in the students. If instructors hold such beliefs, institutional and faculty leaders need to make clear what is happening with the current college student body in such a way that the beliefs can be challenged and hopefully changed. To accomplish this, faculty development based on transformative learning practices (disorienting dilemmas and critical reflection) has been proven effective in challenging the faculty's unexamined beliefs about student learning and faculty roles and encouraging the development of new teaching practices for online and face-to-face classes. And instructors need to be willing to inspect their beliefs and change them if need be. Perhaps some of the engagement strategies discussed earlier will also need to be applied to instructors, as a way to encourage the development of a reflective and engaged instructor.

Help for Administrators

Administrators, be they high-level leaders of the institution or online program managers, have a clear role in improving the student engagement in online learning by making the recommendations above become a reality. Here are seven specific recommendations that only administrators can satisfy.

First, *fund faculty development*. Faculty have to learn new skills and ways of instructing when they go online. They need to better understand learning theories and the various pedagogies available to them. They need help connecting specific pedagogies with learning outcomes as well as to the technologies that can make the activity possible. Faculty may need help identifying engagement strategies for online learning and sharing their findings with other faculty teaching online. And faculty, who likely respect and value research in their discipline, need to understand the evidence for engagement and online pedagogies that can be found in current research journals on online learning.

Second, *fund instructional designers*. Instructional designers have a unique set of skills that can be brought to bear on the development and improvement of online courses. They can help instructors understand the role of theory and pedagogy and perhaps introduce instructors to many more options for achieving their course objectives. Instructional designers help faculty connect pedagogy and technology, and provide many alternatives to consider. This is especially important as adding variety and adjusting to changing student needs or technology advancements will be ever more critical in the future.

Third, *reward innovation*. Online instructors and designers may be pursuing online learning for many reasons, but everyone needs recognition for their exceptional efforts. So rewards may address recognizing the effort needed to learn how to teach online in tenure and promotion decisions or annual evaluations, but they may also include news articles for the institutional community on new developments in online learning achieved by certain faculty or groups of faculty. Putting a program online is a lengthy and challenging endeavor, and offering online courses can also be demanding as the instructor is called upon to provide more help to individual students.

Fourth, *support research into online learning and engagement*. Administrators recognize that faculty value research and learn from it. But the audience for useful research is not just faculty, but other administrators and students. Support might include small grants to fund costs not covered by departments or it may include sharing results through seminars or webinars or listservs.

Fifth, *provide data on students.* Administrators have, and can collect, a wealth of data on the nature of current and incoming students such as the number of students working part time, enrolling part time, or having problems with self-regulation. To be very helpful to instructors, these data need to be for specific degree programs or departments. These data need to be regularly shared with online instructors and designers so that courses can better address student needs. Administrators should also consider collecting additional data on student skills and attitudes so that instructors and designers can develop orientation material, web-based modules, or online courses that enhance those skills needed in online learning.

Sixth, *help students learn how to learn.* Administrators can explore a variety of ways to help students learn how to learn, not just make the transition to college, but how to learn and think and explore ideas. Learning how to learn is a generic need, required by students in various disciplines and programs, be they on campus or online. Such efforts need to be available online so that faculty can refer students to these exercises or modules as an aid to developing their learning in a discipline.

Seventh, *offer online opportunities and programs to help online students attach to the institution.* Although the techniques discussed earlier ought to help online students become engaged in their online courses, NSSE has found that students need various opportunities to interact with institutions in other ways that are also beneficial for developing commitment to the institution. Are student organizations able to include online students? Is there student government for online students? Can online students take advantage of activities online, such as games telecast over the web, debates, or even protests? Administrators may need to evaluate the usefulness of these opportunities in light of their cost and relevance to their online students, and perhaps discussing these services with other institutions that provide them may be helpful.

Future Research

The need for further research affects what instructors, designers, and administrators can do. We know that some approaches (e.g., active learning, tailoring to students, and clear objectives) do work to engage students in their online coursework. But the field of online learning obviously needs more research into what specific engagement strategies work for which students, for which learning objectives, for what disciplines, and for what online settings. Instructors and designers need to move beyond "Does it work?" to why it works and when it does not work. Professionals in the field need research that compares engagement practices so that instructors and designers can choose the best practice that also incorporates an assessment of costs and benefits of engagement practices so that institutions can use scarce resources most effectively. Online learning professionals need specifics and not generalities as well as better data and fewer assertions. For example, instructors and designers need to find out if students with various deficiencies (e.g., a lack of self-discipline, a lack of writing skills, or a lack of generalized learning skills) can overcome those deficiencies, using which engagement strategies, in what kinds of learning situations, and when engagement strategies can be most effectively applied.

The field of online learning also needs to fully explore research on what engagement strategies cannot do, which students may not need them or may not respond positively to them, and what factors may prevent such strategies from working on particular students. The field's knowledge of what engagement strategies work when and for whom needs to grow more granular, more specific, and more prescriptive. Faculty need to undertake research into out-of-class influences on online students to confirm whether or not, or to what extent, these influences impact student engagement, learning, retention, and satisfaction with their online education.

To find these and many other answers, the field needs many online instructors to get involved in this research. This research needs to be conducted as soon as instructors can design different tests of engagement strategies, and the results need to be incorporated into conference presentations, research publications, faculty development programs, and newsletters of the professional organizations that serve the disciplines, professional programs, and the faculty and administrators who teach and manage online programs.

Helpful Directions for the Future

Although this monograph is not about MOOCs (Massively Open Online Courses), the attention placed on them in the current press is reminiscent of the optimistic and impractical views of online learning in its early days. Online learning was going to be the answer to the states' need for increasing state residents' access to higher education, lowering the cost of higher education, and allowing students to learn as quickly as possible so that they would graduate faster. Some of the pundits of the time also implied that online learning could be done by one famous faculty person or no faculty at all. Other supporters seemed to imply that with the Internet, and all of the information being put on the web, students would learn effectively without instructors, institutions, or much effort.

Since these early halcyon days, online learning professionals have learned that online learning can address the needs of many students, but perhaps not all of them. Furthermore, cost issues are not resolved yet, and able instructors with online teaching skills, the ability to diagnose thinking errors, and the passion for students are just as needed as they ever were. One suspects these are some of the lessons that will have to be learned (again) with MOOCs. What makes this odd "back to the future" situation more concerning is the tendency of MOOCs to be experienced by some students passively, viewing videos, listening to lectures, and reading text online. Many MOOCs do not yet emphasize student engagement practices. This may be because the mode of being online is thought to be inherently engaging, or that the technology is always engaging to students, or that students are innately engaged with learning. All of which may be true in part. Or it may be because MOOCs, to serve large numbers of students, cannot use the kinds of active and collaborative learning approaches that encourage engagement because involvement is not required. It may also be the case that engagement will necessarily require greater attention by instructors or tutors or require more instructors or smaller MOOCs, which will make MOOCs less cost-efficient. Currently, it appears that many students enrolled in MOOCs are not inclined to finish the course or to complete all of the exercises. This problem may be resolved as institutions decide how to grant credit for MOOCs, assuming they do more than presume learning has occurred because a student was enrolled. All of these conditions may change as MOOCs evolve and as the instructors and institutions relearn the lessons of online learning and adopt more engagement practices and focus their attention on retention and student learning. In other words, what has made online learning a viable, effective learning approach has been its many years of exploration, testing, and research; years in which a lot of bad courses transformed into better ones and then good ones; and years during which many professionals improved their instructional skills and especially learned how to explicitly address student learning and engagement needs.

Despite its many years of development, online learning is always new to someone: new instructors, new legislators, new parents, and new students. The field of online learning needs to find ways that issues studied in the past are shared with these various groups rather than assuming that research articles published in the literature are the only source of reliable research-based information about online learning. Everyone working in the field of online learning needs to understand that even if online professionals are convinced of its usefulness, those who are new to online learning need to be provided evidence on what it can do and do well (and conversely, what it cannot do well). All of those outside online learning need to be convinced as well. In other words, the work of researchers into online learning—and those who communicate those findings to the public—will never be done. So it is best to get on with this work.

Summary

The focus of this chapter is to identify themes from the research and discussions in the first through fifth chapters. It identifies the learning theories that have the most potential for creating student engagement, advice to instructors to know as much as possible about online students, and the need to help some online students learn how to learn. Instructors need to be clear about what they are doing in online courses and why and share this information with students, understand the possible limits of engagement approaches, be free to seek and explore engagement strategies that may be drawn from pre-Internet research studies or theories, and understand their own philosophies of teaching and learning especially in light of undertaking the development or offering of online coursework. Advice for administrators is provided, stressing funding faculty development and instructional designers, as well as addressing campus-wide needs such as developing modules that help students learn how to learn and providing data on online students to faculty who teach online. Future research studies are discussed that stress the need for more research into specific engagement strategies, disciplines, students, and learning outcomes. Finally, the chapter discusses how MOOCs might consider the adoption of engagement strategies and the need for all faculty and administrators to remember that what we know about online learning needs to be shared with the public, legislatures, and Congress.

For online instructors and designers:

1. Think "active": projects that require students to apply, design, explore, or create.
2. Think "collaborate": assignments that ask students to work with others to complete educational projects.
3. Learn as much about students as possible.
4. Help students learn how to learn.
5. Look for engagement strategies in face-to-face pedagogies.
6. Evaluate engagement strategies and research what works best.

For administrators:

1. Fund and support faculty development and instructional experts.
2. Explore ways the institution can provide basic training in learning how to learn for students new to higher education or online learning.
3. Explore ways to help online students attach to the institution.

For all online educators:

1. Be prepared to provide data on successes.
2. Keep improving what you do.

The hope is for this monograph to provide the interested online educator or administrator with ideas for encouraging more engagement in online learning on the part of students. However, it can only capture what is known about engagement in online learning at the current time, and future research is sorely needed to add specificity to the field's understanding of what works and when and with whom. So please, instructors and designers, design online courses that explore engagement strategies, collect information on what was achieved (or not), and share any findings with others who are working to improve their online offerings. The best way to foster great engagement in online learning is by greater understanding of what works, why, and how. The field of online learning can make progress in improving the experiences of an increasing number of online students through connections between theory and research. Online students deserve courses that help them learn, graduate, and have fruitful and happy lives.

References

Ahlfeldt, S., Mehta, S., & Sellnow, T. (2005). Measurement and analysis of student engagement in university classes where varying levels of PBL methods of instruction are in use. *Higher Education Research & Development*, *24*(1), 5–20.

Akyol, Z., & Garrison, D. R. (2011). Assessing metacognition in an online community of inquiry. *Internet and Higher Education*, *14*, 183–190.

Akyol, Z., Ice, P., Garrison, P., & Mitchell, R. (2010). The relationship between course socio-epistemological orientations and student perceptions of community of inquiry. *Internet and Higher Education*, *13*, 66–68.

Allen, I. E., & Seaman, J. (2012). *Changing course: Ten years of tracking online education in the United States*. Boston, MA: Babson Survey Research Group.

Amador, J. A., & Mederer, H. (2013). Migrating successful student engagement strategies online: Opportunities and challenges using jigsaw groups and problem-based learning. *MERLOT Journal of Online Learning and Teaching*, *9*(1). Retrieved from http://jolt.merlot.org/vol9no1/amador_0313.htm

Anderson, T. (2008). *The theory and practice of online learning*. Edmonton, AB: Athabasca Press.

Angeli, C., Valanides, N., & Bonk, C. (2003). Communication in a web-based conferencing system: The quality of computer-mediated interactions. *British Journal of Educational Technology*, *34*(1), 31–43.

Arbaugh, J. B. (2000). How classroom environment and student engagement affect learning in Internet-based MBA courses. *Business Communication Quarterly*, *63*(4), 9–26.

Arbaugh, J. B. (2001). How instructor immediacy behaviors affect student satisfaction and learning in web-based courses. *Business Communication Quarterly*, *64*(4) 42–54.

Arbaugh, J. B. (2005). Is there an optimal design for on-line MBA courses? *Academy of Management Learning & Education*, *4*, 135–149.

Arbaugh, J. B. (2010). Sage, guide, both, or even more? An examination of instructor activity in online MBA courses. *Computers & Education*, *55*(3), 1234–1244.

Arbaugh, J. B. (2013). Does academic discipline moderate CoI-course outcomes relationships in online MBA courses? *Internet and Higher Education*, *17*, 16–28.

Arbaugh, J. B., & Benbunan-Fich, R. (2006). An investigation of epistemological and social dimensions of teaching in online learning environments. *Management Learning*, *5*(4), 435–447.

Arbaugh, J. B., Cleveland-Innes, M., Diaz, S. R., Garrison, D. R., Ice, P., Richardson, J. C., & Swan, K. P. (2008). Developing a community of inquiry instrument: Testing a measure of the community of inquiry framework using a multi-institutional sample. *Internet and Higher Education, 11*(3–4), 133–136.

Archibald, D. (2010). Fostering the development of cognitive presence: Initial findings using the community of inquiry survey instrument. *Internet and Higher Education, 13*, 73–74.

Arnold, N., & Ducate, L. (2006). Future foreign language teachers' social and cognitive collaboration in an online environment. *Language Learning & Technology, 10*(1), 42–66.

Askov, E. N., & Simpson, M. (2002). Penn State's online adult education M.Ed. degree on the World Campus. *Quarterly Review of Distance Education, 3*(3), 283–294.

Aslanian, C. B., & Clinefelter, D. L. (2013). *Online college students 2013: Comprehensive data on demands and preferences.* Louisville, KY: The Learning House.

Astin, A. W. (1977). *What matters most in college: Four critical years.* San Francisco, CA: Jossey-Bass.

Astin, A. W. (1984). Student involvement: A developmental theory for higher education. *Journal of College Student Personnel, 25*(3), 297–308.

Astin, A. W. (1993a). *What matters most in college: Four critical years revisited.* San Francisco, CA: Jossey-Bass.

Astin, A. W. (1993b). An empirical typology of college students. *Journal of College Student Development, 34*(1), 36–46.

Astin, A. W. (1999). Student involvement: A developmental theory for higher education. *Journal of College Student Development, 40*, 518–529.

Bambara, C. S., Harbour, C. P., Davies, T. G., & Athey, S. (2009). Delicate engagement: The lived experience of community college students enrolled in high-risk online courses. *Community College Review, 36*, 219–238.

Bangert, A. W. (2009). Building a validity argument for the community of inquiry survey instrument. *Internet and Higher Education, 12*, 104–111.

Barkley, E. F. (2010). *Student engagement techniques.* San Francisco, CA: Jossey-Bass.

Bean, J. P., & Metzner, B. S. (1985). A conceptual model of nontraditional undergraduate student attrition. *Review of Educational Research, 55*(4), 485–540.

Benbunan-Fich, R., & Hiltz, S. R. (2003). Mediators of the effectiveness of online courses. *IEEE Transactions on Professional Communication, 46*(4), 298–312.

Bender, T. (2003). *Discussion-based online teaching to enhance student learning: Theory, practice, and assessment.* Sterling, VA: Stylus.

Berge, Z. L. (1999). Interaction in post-secondary web-based learning. *Educational Technology, 39*(1), 5–11.

Berge, Z. L., & Huang, Y. (2004). A model of sustainable student retention: A holistic perspective on the student dropout problem with special attention to e-learning. *DEOSNEWS, 13*(5). Retrieved from http://learningdesign.psu.edu/index.php/section/deos2/volume_13

Bloom, B. S. (1956). *Taxonomy of educational objectives: The classification of educational goals.* New York, NY: Longmans.

Boekaerts, M. (2011). What have we learned about the social context-student engagement link? *Teachers College Record, 113*(2), 375–393.

Boling, E. C., Hough, M., Krinsky, H., Saleem, H., & Stevens, M. (2012). Cutting the distance in distance education: Perspectives on what promotes positive, online learning experiences. *Internet and Higher Education, 15*, 118–126.

Borup, J., West, R. E., & Graham, C. R. (2012). Improving online social presence through asynchronous video. *Internet and Higher Education*, *15*, 195–203.

Boston, W., Ice, P., Díaz, S. R., Richardson, J., Gibson, A. M., & Swan, K. (2009). An exploration of the relationship between indicators of the community of inquiry framework and retention in online programs. *Journal of Asynchronous Learning Networks*, *13*(3), 67–76.

Burgess, M. L. (2009). Using WebCT as a supplemental tool to enhance critical thinking and engagement among developmental reading students. *Journal of College Reading and Learning*, *39*(2), 9–33.

Carini, R. M., Kuh, G. D., & Klein, S. P. (2006). Student engagement and student learning: Testing the linkages. *Research in Higher Education*, *47*(1), 1–32.

Chen, H., & Williams, J. P. (2009). Use of multi-model media and tools in an online information literacy course: College students' attitudes and perceptions. *Journal of Academic Librarianship*, *35*(1), 14–24.

Chen, P. D., Lambert, A. D., & Guidry, K. R. (2010). Engaging online learners: The impact of web-based learning technology on college student engagement. *Computers & Education*, *54*, 1222–1232.

Chen, W., & Looi, C. (2011). Active classroom participation in a Group Scribbles primary science classroom. *British Journal of Educational Technology*, *42*(4), 676–686.

Chen, Y. (2001). Dimensions of transactional distance in the World Wide Web learning environment: A factor analysis. *British Journal of Educational Technology*, *32*(4), 459–470.

Chickering, A. W., & Ehrman, S. C. (1996). Implementing the seven principles: Technology as a lever. *American Association for Higher Education Bulletin*, *10*, 3–6.

Chickering, A. W., & Gamson, Z. F. (1987). Seven principles for good practice in undergraduate education. *AAHE Bulletin*, *May*, 3–7.

Chronicle of Higher Education. (2011, January 24). *State support for higher education continues to fall*. Retrieved from http://chronicle.com/article/Interactive-Map-State -Support/126032/Grapevine

Clark-Ibáñez, M., & Scott, L. (2008). Learning to teach online. *Teaching Sociology*, *36*(1), 34–41.

Coates, H. (2005). Leveraging LMSs to enhance campus-based student engagement. *Educause Quarterly*, *2005*(1). Retrieved from http://net.educause.edu/ir/library/pdf/EQM05110.pdf

Coates, H. (2006). The value of student engagement for higher education quality assurance. *Quality in Higher Education*, *11*(1), 25–36.

Cole, M. (2009). Using wiki technology to support student engagement: Lessons from the trenches. *Computers & Education*, *52*, 141–146.

Conrad, D. (2002a). Deep in the hearts of learners: Insights into the nature of online community. *Journal of Distance Education*, *17*(1). Retrieved from http://www.ijede.ca/index.php/jde/article/view/133/114

Conrad, D. (2002b). Inhibition, integrity and etiquette among online learners: The art of niceness. *Distance Education*, *23*(2), 197–212.

Conrad, D. (2002c). Engagement, excitement, anxiety, and fear: Learners' experiences of starting an online course. *LEA Online*, *16*(4), 205–226.

Conrad, R., & Donaldson, J. A. (2011). *Engaging the online learner*. San Francisco, CA: Jossey-Bass.

Conrad, R., & Donaldson, J. A. (2012). *Continuing to engage the online learner*. San Francisco, CA: Jossey-Bass.

Coole, H., & Watts, M. (2009). Communal e-learning styles in the online classroom. *Research in Education, 82*, 13–27.

Corno, L., & Mandinach, E. B. (1983). The role of cognitive engagement in classroom learning and motivation. *Educational Psychologist, 18*(2), 88–108.

Cross, K. P. (1998). Why learning communities? Why now? *About Campus, 3*(3), 4–11. Retrieved from http://www.nhcuc.org/pdfs/CrossLC.pdf

Davies, J., & Graff, M. (2005). Performance in e-learning: Online participation and student grades. *British Journal of Educational Technology, 36*, 657–663.

Dewey, J. (1910). *How we think.* Boston, MA: D. C. Heath.

Díaz, S. R., Swan, K., Ice, P., & Kupczynski, L. (2010). Student ratings of the importance of survey items, multiplicative factor analysis, and the validity of the community of inquiry survey. *Internet and Higher Education, 13*, 22–30.

Dick, W., Carey, L., & Carey, J. O. (2005). *The systematic design of instruction* (6th ed.). New York, NY: Allyn & Bacon.

DiRamio, D., & Wolverton, M. (2006). Integrating learning communities and distance education: Possibility or pipedream? *Innovative Higher Education, 31*(2), 99–113.

Dykman, C., & Davis, C. (2008). Online education forum—Part three: A quality online educational experience. *Journal of Information Systems Education, 19*(3), 281–289.

Dziuban, C., Moskal, P., Cavanagh, T., & Watts, A. (2012). Analytics that inform the university: Using data you already have. *Journal of Asynchronous Learning Networks, 16*(3), 21–38.

Eke, K. J. (2008). Using clickstream recording to make learning visible. *Distance Education Report, 12*(17), 5–7.

Fahy, P. J., Crawford, G., & Ally, M. (2001). Patterns of interaction in a computer conference transcript. *International Review of Open and Distance Learning, 2*(1). Retrieved from http://www.irrodl.org/index.php/irrodl/article/view/36/73

Fisher, K. (2010). Online student engagement: CCSSE finds enrollment status and online experience are key. *Community College Week, 22*(20), 7.

Fu, F., Wu, Y., & Ho, H. (2009). An investigation of coopetitive pedagogic design for knowledge creation in web-based learning. *Computers & Education, 53*(3), 550–562.

Gagné, R. M. (1985). *The conditions of learning* (4th ed.). New York, NY: Holt, Rinehart & Winston.

Gallini, J. K., & Barron, D. D. (2001/2002). Participants' perceptions of web-infused environments: A survey of teaching beliefs, learning approaches, and communication. *Journal of Research on Technology in Education, 34*(2), 139–156.

Gardner, H. (1983). *Frames of mind: The theory of multiple intelligences.* New York, NY: Basic Books.

Garrison, D. R. (2000). Theoretical challenges for distance education in the 21st century: A shift from structural to transactional issues. *International Review of Research in Open and Distance Learning, 1*(1). Retrieved from http://www.irrodl.org/index.php/irrodl/article/viewArticle/2

Garrison, D. R. (2011). *E-Learning in the 21st century: A framework for research and practice* (2nd ed.). London, UK: Routledge.

Garrison, D. R., Anderson, T., & Archer, W. (2000). Critical inquiry in a text-based environment: Computer conferencing in higher education. *Internet and Higher Education, 2*(2–3), 87–105.

Garrison, D. R., Anderson, T., & Archer, W. (2010). The first decade of the community of inquiry framework: A retrospective. *Internet and Higher Education, 13*, 5–9.

Garrison, D. R., & Arbaugh, J. B. (2007). Researching the community of inquiry framework: Review, issues, and future directions. *Internet and Higher Education, 10*(3), 157–172.

Garrison, D. R., & Cleveland-Innes, M. (2005). Facilitating cognitive presence in online learning: Interaction is not enough. *American Journal of Distance Education, 19*(3), 133–148.

Garrison, D. R., Cleveland-Innes, M., & Fung, T. S. (2010). Exploring causal relationships among teaching, cognitive, and social presence: Student perceptions of the community of inquiry framework. *Internet and Higher Education, 13*, 31–36.

Gellin, A. (2003). The effect of undergraduate student involvement on critical thinking: A meta-analysis of the literature, 1991–2000. *Journal of College Student Development, 44*, 746–762.

Gilbert, J., Morton, S., & Rowley, J. (2007). E-learning: The student experience. *British Journal of Educational Technology, 38*, 560–573.

Gilmore, S., & Warren, S. (2007). Emotion online: Experiences of teaching in a virtual learning environment. *Human Relations, 60*(4), 581–608.

Hadwin, A., & Oshige, M. (2011). Self-regulation, co-regulation, and socially shared regulation: Exploring perspectives of social in self-regulated learning theory. *Teachers College Record, 113*(6), 240–264.

Harasim, L. (1990). Online education: An environment for collaboration and intellectual amplification. In L. Harasim (Ed.), *Online education: Perspectives on a new environment* (pp. 39–66). New York, NY: Praeger.

Harper, S. R., & Quaye, S. J. (2009). *Student engagement in higher education: Theoretical perspectives and practical approaches for diverse populations.* New York, NY: Routledge.

Hatch, D. K. (2012). Unpacking the black box of student engagement: The need for programmatic investigation of high impact practices. *Community College Journal of Research and Practice, 36*(11), 903–915.

Herrington, J., Oliver, R., & Reeves, T. C. (2003). Patterns of engagement in authentic online learning environments. *Australian Journal of Educational Technology, 19*(1), 59–71.

Hoffman, B., & Ritchie, D. (1997). Using multimedia to overcome the problems with problem based learning. *Instructional Science, 25*, 97–115.

Holley, D., & Oliver, M. (2010). Student engagement and blended learning: Portraits of risk. *Computers & Education, 54*(3), 693–700.

Hu, S., & Kuh, G. D. (2001). Computing experience and good practices in undergraduate education: Does the degree of campus "wiredness" matter? *Education Policy Analysis Archives, 9*(49). Retrieved from http://epaa.asu.edu/ojs/article/view/378

Hu, S., & McCormick, A. C. (2012). An engagement-based student typology and its relationship to college outcomes. *Research in Higher Education, 53*, 738–754.

Hughes, G. (2005). Learning to learn online: Fostering student engagement with online pedagogies. In P. Hartley, A. Woods, & M. Pill (Eds.), *Enhancing teaching in higher-education: New approaches for improving student learning* (pp. 69–79). London, UK: Routledge.

Jenkins, R. (2011, May 22). Why are so many students still failing online? *The Chronicle of Higher Education.* Retrieved from http://chronicle.com/article/Why-Are-So-Many-Students-Still/127584/

Junco, R., Heiberger, G., & Loken, E. (2010). The effect of Twitter on college student engagement and grades. *Journal of Computer Assisted Learning, 27*(2), 119–132.

Kanuka, H., & Anderson, T. (1998). Online social interchange, discord, and knowledge construction. *Journal of Distance Education, 13*(1). Retrieved from http://www.ijede.ca/index.php/jde/article/view/137/412

Kanuka, H., Rourke, L., & Laflamme, E. (2007). The influence of instructional methods on the quality of online discussions. *British Journal of Educational Technology, 38*(2), 260–271.

Kay, R. H. (2006). Developing a comprehensive metric for assessing discussion board effectiveness. *British Journal of Educational Technology, 37*, 761–783.

Kelderman, E. (2013, January 21). State spending on higher education rebounds in most states after years of decline. *The Chronicle of Higher Education.* Retrieved from http://chronicle.com/article/State-Spending-on-Higher/136745/

Kiley, K. (2013, January 17). Nowhere to turn. *InsideHigherEd.com.* Retrieved from http://www.insidehighered.com/news/2013/01/17/moodys-report-calls-question-all-traditional-university-revenue-sources

Koh, J. H. L., Herring, S. C., & Hew, K. F. (2010). Project-based learning and student knowledge construction during asynchronous online discussion. *Internet and Higher Education, 13*, 284–291.

Kolb, D. (1984). *Experiential learning: Experience as the source of learning and development.* Englewood Cliffs, NJ: Prentice Hall.

Kuh, G. D. (2007). What student engagement data tell us about college readiness. *Association of American Colleges and Universities, 9*(1). Retrieved from http://www.aacu.org/peerreview/pr-wi07/pr-wi07_analysis1.cfm

Kuh, G. D. (2008). *High-impact educational practices: What they are, who has access to them, and why they matter.* Washington, DC: Association of American Colleges and Universities.

Kuh, G. D. (2009). The national survey of student engagement: Conceptual and empirical foundations. In R. M. Gonyea & G. D. Kuh (Eds.), *New Directions for Institutional Research: No. 141. Using NSSE in institutional research* (pp. 5–20). San Francisco, CA: Jossey-Bass.

Kuh, G. D., Cruce, T. M., Shoup, R., Kinzie, J., & Gonyea, R. M. (2008). Unmasking the effects of student engagement on first-year college grades and persistence. *The Journal of Higher Education, 79*(5), 540–563.

Kuh, G. D., & Hu, S. (2001). The relationships between computer and information technology use, student learning, and other college experiences. *Journal of College Student Development, 42*, 217–232.

Kuh, G. D., Hu, S., & Vesper, N. (2000). "They shall be known by what they do": An activities based typology of college students. *Journal of College Student Development, 41*(2), 228–244.

LaPointe, L., & Reisetter, M. (2008). Belonging online: Students' perceptions of the value and efficacy of an online learning community. *International Journal of E-Learning, 7*(4), 641–665.

Layne, M., Boston, W. E., & Ice, P. (2013). A longitudinal study of online learners: Shoppers, swirlers, stoppers, and succeeders as a function of demographic characteristics. *Online Journal of Distance Learning Administration, 16*(2). Retrieved from http://www.westga.edu/˜distance/ojdle/summer162/layne_boston_ice162.html

Lease, M. (2009). Out of class—out of mind? The use of a virtual learning environment to encourage student engagement in out of class activities. *British Journal of Educational Technology, 40*(1), 70–77.

Lemak, D., Shin, S., Reed, R., & Montgomery, J. (2005). Technology, transactional distance, and instructor effectiveness: An empirical investigation. *Academy of Management Learning & Education, 4*(2), 150–158.

Lester, J., & Perini, M. (2010). Potential of social networking sites for distance education student engagement. In R. L. G. Mitchell (Ed.), *New Directions for Community Colleges: No. 150. Online education* (pp. 67–77). San Francisco, CA: Jossey-Bass.

Lewin, K. (1952). *Field theory in social science: Selected theoretical papers by Kurt Lewin*. London, UK: Tavistock.

Lowenthal, P. R., & Dunlap, J. C. (2010). From pixel on a screen to real person in your students' lives: Establishing social presence using digital storytelling. *Internet and Higher Education, 13*, 70–72.

MacGregor, J., Smith, B. L., Tinto, V., & Levine, J. (1999). *Learning about learning communities: Taking student learning seriously*. Paper presented at the meeting of the National Teleconference on Learning Communities, Columbia, SC.

Mason, R. B. (2011). Student engagement with, and participation in, an e-forum. *Educational Technology & Society, 14*(2), 258–268.

McBrien, J. L., Jones, P., & Cheng, R. (2009). Virtual spaces: Employing a synchronous online classroom to facilitate student engagement in online learning. *International Review of Research in Open and Distance Learning, 10*(3). Retrieved from http://www.irrodl.org/index.php/irrodl/article/view/605/1298

McCaslin, M., & Burross, H. L. (2011). Research on individual differences within a sociocultural perspective: Coregulation and adaptive learning. *Teachers College Record, 113*(6), 325–349.

McQuiggan, C. A. (2012). Faculty development for online teaching as a catalyst for change. *Journal of Asynchronous Learning Networks, 12*(1), 27–62.

Merriam, S. B. (2004). The role of cognitive development in Mezirow's transformational learning theory. *Adult Education Quarterly, 55*(1), 60–68.

Metzner, B. S., & Bean, J. (1987). The estimation of a conceptual model of nontraditional undergraduate student attrition. *Research in Higher Education, 27*, 15–38.

Meyer, K. A. (2002). *Quality in distance education: Focus on on-line learning* [ASHE-ERIC Higher Education Report Series, 29(4)]. San Francisco, CA: Jossey-Bass.

Meyer, K. A. (2003). Face-to-face versus threaded discussions: The role of time and higher-order thinking. *Journal of Asynchronous Learning Networks, 7*(3). Retrieved from http://onlinelearningconsortium.org/jaln/v7n3/face-face-versus-threaded-discussions-role-time-and-higher-order-thinking

Meyer, K. A. (2004a). Evaluating online discussions: Four different frames of analysis. *Journal of Asynchronous Learning Networks, 8*(2). Retrieved from http://onlinelearning consortium.org/jaln/v8n2/evaluating-online-discussions-four-different-frames-analysis

Meyer, K. A. (2004b). Putting the distance learning comparison study in perspective: Its role as personal journey research. *The Online Journal of Distance Learning Administration, 7*(1). Retrieved from http://www.westga.edu/˜distance/ojdla/spring71/meyer71.html

Meyer, K. A. (2005). The ebb and flow of online discussions: What Bloom can tell us about our students' conversations. *Journal of Asynchronous Learning Networks, 9*(1), 53–63.

Meyer, K. A. (2012a). The case for the Community of Inquiry (CoI) influencing student retention. In R. Garrison & Z. Aykol (Eds.), *Educational communities of inquiry: Theoretical framework, research and practice* (pp. 317–333). Hershey, PA: IGI Global.

Meyer, K. A. (2012b). Creative uses of discussion boards: Going beyond the ordinary. *The Community College Enterprise, 18*(2), 117–121.

Meyer, K. A. (2014). How community college faculty members may improve student learning productivity in their online courses. *Community College Journal of Research and Practice, 38*(6), 575–587. doi:10.1080/10668926.2012.676501

Meyer, K. A., Bruwelheide, J., & Poulin, R. (2006). Why they stayed: Near-perfect retention in an online certification program in library media. *Journal of Asynchronous Learning Networks, 10*(4), 99–115.

Meyer, K. A., & McNeal, L. (2011). How online faculty improve student learning productivity. *Journal of Asynchronous Learning Networks, 15*(3), 37–53.

Meyer, K. A., & Murrell, V. (2014). A national study of training content and activities for faculty development for online teaching. *Journal of Asynchronous Learning Networks, 18*(1). Retrieved from http://onlinelearningconsortium.org/jaln/v18n1/national-study-training-content-and-activities-faculty-development-online-teaching

Meyers, S. A. (2008). Using transformative pedagogy when teaching online. *College Teaching, 56*(4), 219–224.

Mezirow, J. (1991). *Transformative dimensions of adult learning.* San Francisco, CA: Jossey-Bass.

Moore, M. G. (1972). Learner autonomy: The second dimension of independent learning. *Convergence, 2,* 76–88.

Moore, M. G. (1973). Toward a theory of independent learning and teaching. *Journal of Higher Education, 44*(9), 661–679.

Moore, M. G. (1989). Three types of interaction. *The American Journal of Distance Education, 3*(2), 1–6.

Moore, M. G. (1990). Recent contributions to the theory of distance education. *Open Learning, 5*(3), 10–15.

Moore, M. G. (1991). Editorial: Distance education theory. *The American Journal of Distance Education, 5*(3), 1–6.

Moore, M. G. (2007). The theory of transactional distance. In M. G. Moore (Ed.), *Handbook of distance education* (2nd ed., pp. 89–105). Mahway, NJ: Lawrence Erlbaum Associates.

Murphy, E. (2004). Identifying and measuring ill-structured problem formulation and resolution in online asynchronous discussions. *Canadian Journal of Learning and Technology, 30*(1), 5–20.

Nagel, L., & Kotzé, T. (2010). Supersizing e-learning: What a CoI survey reveals about teaching presence in a large online class. *The Internet and Higher Education, 13*(1–2), 45–51.

National Center for Education Statistics (NCES). (2010). *Table 38.* Retrieved from http://nces.ed.gov/datalab/tableslibrary/viewtable.aspx?tableid=7512

National Center for Education Statistics (NCES). (2011a). *Enrollment in postsecondary institutions, fall 2009; graduation rates, 2003 & 2006 cohorts; and financial statistics, fiscal year 2009.* Retrieved from http://nces.ed.gov/pubs2011/2011230.pdf

National Center for Education Statistics (NCES). (2011b). *Condition of Education 2011.* Retrieved from http://nces.ed.gov/pubs2011/2011033_6.pdf

National Center for Education Statistics (NCES). (2012). *Enrollment in postsecondary institutions, fall 2011; Financial statistics, fiscal year 2011; and graduation rates, selected cohorts, 2003–2008.* Retrieved from http://nces.ed.gov/pubs2012/2012174rev.pdf

Nelson Laird, T. F., & Kuh, G. D. (2005). Student experiences with information technology and their relationship to other aspects of student engagement. *Research in Higher Education, 46*(2), 211–233.

Nora, A. (2003). Access to higher education for Hispanic students: Real or illusory? In J. Castellanos & L. Jones (Eds.), *The majority in the minority: Expanding the representation of Latina/o faculty, administrators and students in higher education* (pp. 47–68). Sterling, VA: Stylus.

Oren, A., Mioduser, D., & Nachmias, R. (2002). The development of social climate in virtual learning discussion groups. *International Review of Research in Open and Distance Learning, 3*(1). Retrieved from http://www.irrodl.org/index.php/irrodl/article/view/80/155

Pace, C. R. (1980). Measuring the quality of student effort. *Current Issues in Higher Education, 2*, 10–16.

Palloff, R. M., & Pratt, K. (1999). *Building learning communities in cyberspace*. San Francisco, CA: Jossey-Bass.

Pascarella, E. T., & Terenzini, P. T. (1991). *How college affects students: Findings and insights from 20 years of research*. San Francisco, CA: Jossey-Bass.

Pascarella, E. T., & Terenzini, P. T. (2005). *How college affects students: A third decade of research*. San Francisco, CA: Jossey-Bass.

Paulus, T. M., Horvitz, B., & Shi, M. (2006). "Isn't it just like our situation?" Engagement and learning in an online story-based environment. *Educational Technology Research & Development, 54*(4), 355–385.

Pawan, F., Paulus, T. M., Yalcin, S., & Chang, C. (2003). Online learning: Patterns of engagement and interaction among in-service teachers. *Language Learning & Technology, 7*(3), 119–140.

Perry, B. (2006). Using photographic images as an interactive online teaching strategy. *Internet and Higher Education, 9*, 229–240.

Peters, L., Shmerling, S., & Karren, R. (2011). Constructivist pedagogy in asynchronous online education: Examining proactive behavior and the impact on student engagement levels. *International Journal of E-Learning, 10*(3), 311–330.

Picciano, A. G. (2012). The evolution of big data and learning analytics in American higher education. *Journal of Asynchronous Learning Networks, 16*(3), 9–20.

Pike, G. R., & Kuh, G. D. (2005). A typology of student engagement for American colleges and universities. *Research in Higher Education, 46*, 185–210.

Preece, J., Nonnecke, B., & Andrews, D. (2004). The top five reasons for lurking: Improving community experiences for everyone. *Computers in Human Behavior, 20*(2), 201–223.

Pyrtle, A. J., Powell, J. M., & Williamson-Whitney, V. A. (2007). Virtual community building for effective engagement of students of color in earth system science: Minorities striving and pursuing higher degrees of success in earth science case study. *Journal of Geoscience Education, 55*(6), 522–530.

Ragan, L. (1999). Good teaching is good teaching: An emerging set of guiding principles and practices for the design and development of distance education. *CAUSE/EFFECT, 22*(1). Retrieved from http://net.educause.edu/ir/library/html/cem/cem99/cem9915.html

Reynolds, J. (1995). Indicators of educational effectiveness. In S. Hatfield (Ed.), *The seven principles in action: Improving undergraduate education* (pp. 107–114). Boston, MA: Anker Publishing.

Richardson, J. C., & Ice, P. (2010). Investigating students' level of critical thinking across instructional strategies in online discussions. *Internet and Higher Education, 13*, 52–59.

Richardson, J. C., & Newby, T. (2006). The role of students' cognitive engagement in online learning. *American Journal of Distance Education, 20*(1), 23–37.

Richardson, J. C., & Swan, K. (2003). Examining social presence in online courses in relation to students' perceived learning and satisfaction. *Journal of Asynchronous Learning Networks, 7*(1), 68–88.

Robinson, C., & Hullinger, H. (2008). New benchmarks in higher education: Student engagement in online learning. *Journal of Education for Business, 84*(2), 101–108.

Robinson, J. (2010). Assessing the value of using an online discussion board for engaging students. *Journal of Hospitality, Leisure, Sport & Tourism Education, 10*(1), 13–22. doi: 10.3794/johlste.101.257

Romero, M., & Barberà, E. (2011). Quality of learners' time and learning performance beyond quantitative time-on-task. *The International Review of Research in Open and Distance Learning, 12*(5), 126–137.

Rose, R. (2012, May 31). 6 keys to engaging students online. *Campus Technology*. Retrieved from http://campustechnology.com/articles/2012/05/31/6-keys-to-engaging-students-online.aspx

Rourke, L., & Anderson, T. (2004). Validity in quantitative content analysis. *Educational Technology Research and Development, 52*(1), 5–18.

Rourke, L., Anderson, T., Garrison, D. R., & Archer, W. (2001). Assessing social presence in asynchronous, text-based computer conferencing. *Journal of Distance Education, 14*(3), 51–70.

Rourke, L., & Kanuka, H. (2009). Learning in communities of inquiry: A review of the literature. *International Journal of E-Learning and Distance Education, 23*(1), 19–48.

Rovai, A. P. (2002a). Development of an instrument to measure classroom community. *Internet and Higher Education, 5*(3), 197–211.

Rovai, A. P. (2002b). Sense of community, perceived cognitive learning, and persistence in asynchronous learning networks. *Internet and Higher Education, 5*(4), 319–322.

Rovai, A. P. (2003). In search of higher persistence rates in distance education online programs. *Internet and Higher Education, 6*, 1–16.

Rubin, B., Fernandes, R., & Avgerinou, M. D. (2013). The effects of technology on the community of inquiry and satisfaction with online courses. *Internet and Higher Education, 17*, 48–57.

Russell, T. L. (1999). *No significant difference phenomenon*. Raleigh: North Carolina State University.

Schilling, K. (2009). The impact of multimedia course enhancements on student learning outcomes. *Journal of Education for Library and Information Science, 50*(4), 214–225.

Schrand, T. (2008). Tapping into active learning and multiple intelligences with interactive multimedia. *College Teaching, 56*(2), 78–84.

Schulte, M., Dennis, K., Eskey, M., Taylor, C., & Zeng, H. (2012). Creating a sustainable online instructor observation system: A case study highlighting flaws when blending mentoring and evaluation. *International Review of Research in Open and Distance Learning, 13*(3), 83–96.

Shea, P. (2006). A study of students' sense of learning community in online environments. *Journal of Asynchronous Learning Networks, 10*(1), 35–44.

Shea, P., & Bidjerano, T. (2009). Community of inquiry as a theoretical framework to foster "epistemic engagement" and "cognitive presence" in online education. *Computers and Education, 52*(3), 543–553.

Shea, P., Hayes, S., Smith, S. U., Vickers, J., Bidjerano, T., Pickett, A., . . . Jian, S. (2012). Learning presence: Additional research on a new conceptual element within the community of inquiry (CoI) framework. *Internet and Higher Education, 15*, 89–95.

Shea, P., Hayes, S., Vickers, J., Gozza-Cohen, M., Uzuner, S., Mehta, R., . . . Rangan, P. (2010). A re-examination of the community of inquiry framework: Social network and content analysis. *Internet and Higher Education, 13*, 10–21.

Shea, P., Li, C. S., & Pickett, A. (2006). A study of teaching presence and student sense of learning community in fully online and web-enhanced college courses. *Internet and Higher Education, 9*(3), 175–190.

Shea, P., Pickett, A., & Li, C. S. (2005). Increasing access to higher education: A study of the diffusion of online teaching among 913 college faculty. *International Review of Research in Open and Distance Learning, 6*(2), 1–27.

Sherer, P., & Shea, T. (2011). Using online video to support student learning and engagement. *College Teaching, 59*(2), 56–59.

Sheridan, K., & Kelly, M. A. (2010). The indicators of instructor presence that are important to students in online courses. *MERLOT Journal of Online Learning and Teaching, 6*(4), 767–779.

Sherrill, J. (2012). *22 variables that don't affect retention of online or dev ed courses anywhere (and a few that do)*. Retrieved from http://wcet.wiche.edu/wcet/docs/par/22Variables NotAffectingRetentionofOnlineStudents_SHerrill_April18-2012.pdf

Shin, N., & Chan, J. K. Y. (2004). Direct and indirect effects of online learning on distance education. *British Journal of Educational Technology, 35*(3), 275–288.

Siemens, G., & Long, P. (2011). Penetrating the fog: Analytics in learning and education. *EDUCAUSE Review, 46*(5). Retrieved from http://www.educause.edu/ero/article/penetrating-fog-analytics-learning-and-education

Song, L., Singleton, E. S., Hill, J. R., & Koh, M. H. (2004). Improving online learning: Student perceptions of useful and challenging characteristics. *Internet and Higher Education, 7*, 59–70.

Stefanou, C. R., Perencevich, K. C., DiCintio, M., & Turner, J. C. (2004). Supporting autonomy in the classroom: Ways teachers encourage student decision making and ownership. *Educational Psychologist, 39*(2), 97–110.

Stein, D. S., Wanstreet, C. E., Slagle, P., Trinko, L. A., & Lutz, M. (2013). From "hello" to higher-order thinking: The effect of coaching and feedback on online chats. *Internet and Higher Education, 16*, 78–84.

Strickland, A. W. (n.d.). *ADDIE*. Retrieved from http://web.archive.org/web/20060709 154016/http://ed.isu.edu/addie/index.html

Sullivan, F. R., Hamilton, C. E., Allessio, D. A., Boit, R. J., Deschamps, A. D., Sindelar, T., . . . Zhu, Y. (2011). Representational guidance and student engagement: Examining designs for collaboration in online synchronous environments. *Educational Technology Research & Development, 59*(5), 619–644.

Sun, J. C., & Rueda, R. (2012). Situational interest, computer self-efficacy and self-regulation: Their impact on student engagement in distance education. *British Journal of Educational Technology, 43*(2), 191–204.

Sutton, S. C., & Nora, A. (2008–2009). An exploration of college persistence for students enrolled in web-enhanced courses: A multivariate analytic approach. *Journal of College Student Retention, 10*(1), 21–37.

Swan, K. (2001). Virtual interaction: Design factors affecting student satisfaction and perceived learning in asynchronous online courses. *Distance Education, 22*(2), 306–331.

Swan, K., Matthews, D., Bogle, L., Boles, E., & Day, S. (2012). Linking online course design and implementation to learning outcomes: A design experiment. *Internet and Higher Education, 15*, 81–88.

Tandberg, D., & Hillman, N. (2013). *State performance funding for higher education: Silver bullet or red herring?* (WISCAPE Policy Brief 18). Madison: University of Wisconsin-Madison, Wisconsin Center for the Advancement of Postsecondary Education (WISCAPE).

Taplin, M. (2000). Problem-based learning in distance education: Practitioners' beliefs about an action learning project. *Distance Education, 21*(2), 284–307.

Thompson, T. L., & MacDonald, C. J. (2005). Community building, emergent design and expecting the unexpected: Creating a quality eLearning experience. *Internet and Higher Education, 8*(3), 233–249.

Tinto, V. (1987). *Leaving college: Rethinking the causes and cures of student attrition.* Chicago, IL: University of Chicago Press.

Tinto, V. (1998). Colleges as communities: Taking research on student persistence seriously. *Review of Higher Education, 21*(2), 167–177.

Tobias, S., & Everson, H. T. (2009). The importance of knowing what you know: A knowledge monitoring framework for studying metacognition in education. In D. L. Hacker, J. Dunlosky, & A. Graesser (Eds.), *Handbook of metacognition in education* (pp. 107–128). New York, NY: Routledge.

Umbach, P. D., & Wawrzynski, M. R. (2005). Faculty do matter: The role of college faculty in student learning and engagement. *Research in Higher Education, 46*(2), 153–184.

Vaughan, N. D. (2004). *Investigating how a blended learning approach can support an inquiry process within a faculty learning community* (Unpublished doctoral dissertation). University of Calgary, Canada.

Vaughan, N. D. (2010). A blended community of inquiry approach: Linking student engagement and course redesign. *Internet and Higher Education, 13*, 60–65.

Waldner, L., McGorry, S., & Widener, M. (2010). Extreme e-service learning (XE-SL): E-service learning in the 100% online course. *MERLOT Journal of Online Learning and Teaching, 6*(4), 839–851.

Wankel, C., & Blessinger, P. (2012). *Increasing student engagement and retention using online learning activities: Wikis, blogs, and WebQuests.* Bingley, UK: Emerald Group Publishing.

Wegerif, R. (1998). The social dimension of asynchronous learning networks. *Journal of Asynchronous Learning Networks, 2*(1), 34–49.

WICHE Cooperative for Educational Telecommunications. (2013). *Managing online education 2013: Practices in ensuring quality.* Retrieved from http://wcet.wiche.edu/advance/managing-online-education-survey

Williams, J., & Chinn, S. J. (2009). Using Web 2.0 to support the active learning experience. *Journal of Information Systems Education, 20*(2), 165–174.

Wilson, G. (2004). Online interaction impacts on learning: Teaching the teaching to teach online. *Australasian Journal of Educational Technology, 20*(1), 33–48.

Xu, Y. (2010). Examining the effects of digital feedback on student engagement and achievement. *Journal of Educational Computing Research, 43*(3), 275–291.

Zach, L., & Agosto, D. E. (2009). Using the online learning environment to develop real-life collaboration and knowledge-sharing skills: A theoretical discussion and framework for online course design. *MERLOT Journal of Online Learning and Teaching, 5*(4), 590–599.

Zhao, C., & Kuh, G. D. (2004). Adding value: Learning communities and student engagement. *Research in Higher Education, 45*(2), 115–138.

Zhu, E. (1998). Learning and mentoring: Electronic discussion in a distance learning course. In C. Bonk & K. King (Eds.), *Electronic collaborators: Learner-centered technologies for literacy, apprenticeship, and discourse* (pp. 233–259). Hillsdale, NJ: Lawrence Erlbaum Associates.

Zhu, E. (2006). Interaction and cognitive engagement: An analysis of four asynchronous online discussions. *Instructional Science, 34*(6), 451–480.

Name Index

A

Agosto, D. E., 31
Ahlfeldt, S., 45
Akyol, Z., 25, 27
Allen, I. E., 2, 10
Allessio, D. A., 57
Ally, M., 20, 42
Amador, J. A., 45
Anderson, T., 16, 20, 21, 26, 27, 80
Andrews, D., 78
Angeli, C., 82
Arbaugh, J. B., 17, 21, 22, 23, 25, 70, 71, 80, 83
Archer, W., 16, 20, 21
Archibald, D., 21
Arnold, N., 20
Askov, E. N., 70
Aslanian, C. B., 11
Astin, A. W., 5, 6, 68, 75, 79
Athey, S., 70
Avgerinou, M. D., 60

B

Bambara, C. S., 70
Bangert, A. W., 17
Barberà, E., 69, 76
Barkley, E. F., 63
Barron, D. D., 27
Bean, J. P., 5, 23
Benbunan-Fich, R., 21, 70, 71
Bender, T., 43

Berge, Z. L., 23, 43
Bidjerano, T., 17, 19, 22, 24
Blessinger, P., 60
Bloom, B. S., 42
Boekaerts, M., 77, 78
Bogle, L., 19, 22, 71, 84
Boit, R. J., 57
Boles, E., 19, 22, 71, 84
Boling, E. C., 39, 59
Bonk, C., 82
Borup, J., 21
Boston, W. E., 19, 49, 77
Bruwelheide, J., 23, 71
Burgess, M. L., 58
Burross, H. L., 78

C

Carey, J. O., 53
Carey, L., 53
Carini, R. M., 68
Cavanagh, T., 48
Chan, J. K. Y., 50, 70, 71
Chang, C., 20
Chen, H., 58
Chen, P. D., 9, 35
Chen, W., 38
Chen, Y., 35
Cheng, R., 81
Chickering, A. W., 7
Chinn, S. J., 28, 59
Clark-Ibáñez, M., 84

J

Jenkins, R., 4
Jian, S., 24
Jones, P., 81
Junco, R., 60

K

Kanuka, H., 20, 27, 71
Karren, R., 28, 76
Kay, R. H., 81
Kelderman, E., 3
Kelly, M. A., 46, 47, 81
Kiley, K., 3
Kinzie, J., 61, 68
Klein, S. P., 68
Koh, J. H. L., 28
Koh, M. H., 49, 79
Kolb, D., 28
Kotze, T., 23
Krinsky, H., 39, 59
Kuh, G. D., 6, 10, 32, 33, 46, 50, 61, 68, 69, 79
Kupczynski, L., 17, 19, 21

L

Laflamme, E., 20
Lambert, A. D., 9
LaPointe, L., 32
Layne, M., 49, 77
Lease, M., 50
Lemak, D., 35
Lester, J., 59, 63
Levine, J., 32
Lewin, K., 15
Li, C. S., 23, 83
Loken, E., 60
Long, P., 48
Looi, C., 38
Lowenthal, P. R., 21
Lutz, M., 47, 70

M

MacDonald, C. J., 31
MacGregor, J., 32
Mandinach, E. B., 33

Mason, R. B., 79, 82
Matthews, D., 19, 22, 71, 84
McBrien, J. L., 81
McCaslin, M., 78
McCormick, A. C., 8, 79
McGorry, S., 45
McNeal, L., 34, 39, 44
McQuiggan, C. A., 30
Mederer, H., 45
Mehta, R., 21, 42, 82
Mehta, S., 45
Merriam, S. B., 29
Metzner, B. S., 5, 23
Meyer, K. A., 4, 19, 23, 24, 27, 30, 34, 39, 41, 42, 44, 52, 70, 71, 80, 84
Meyers, S. A., 29, 44, 46
Mezirow, J., 29
Mioduser, D., 31
Mitchell, R., 27
Montgomery, J., 35
Moore, M. G., 13, 34, 37, 38, 40
Morton, S., 78
Moskal, P., 48
Murphy, E., 20
Murrell, V., 30

N

Nachmias, R., 31
Nagel, L., 23
Nelson Laird, T. F., 10
Newby, T., 33, 49, 70
Nonnecke, B., 78
Nora, A., 7

O

Oliver, M., 51
Oliver, R., 29, 45
Oren, A., 31
Oshige, M., 77

P

Pace, C. R., 6
Palloff, R. M., 30, 31
Pascarella, E. T., 7, 68, 75
Paulus, T. M., 20, 45, 70

Pawan, F., 20
Perencevich, K. C., 51
Perini, M., 59, 63
Perry, B., 58
Peters, L., 28, 76
Picciano, A. G., 48
Pickett, A., 23, 24, 83
Pike, G. R., 68
Poulin, R., 23, 71
Powell, J. M., 77
Pratt, K., 30, 31
Preece, J., 78
Pyrtle, A. J., 77

Q

Quaye, S. J., 61

R

Ragan, L., 84
Rangan, P., 21, 42, 82
Reed, R., 35
Reeves, T. C., 29, 45
Reisetter, M., 32
Reynolds, J., 51
Richardson, J. C., 17, 19, 22, 33, 43, 49, 70
Ritchie, D., 77
Robinson, C., 9
Robinson, J., 71
Romero, M., 69, 76
Rose, R., 80
Rourke, L., 20, 21, 26, 71
Rovai, A. P., 23, 31
Rowley, J., 78
Rubin, B., 60
Rueda, R., 50, 69
Russell, T. L., 58

S

Saleem, H., 59
Schilling, K., 39, 58
Schrand, T., 28
Schulte, M., 83
Scott, L., 84
Seaman, J., 2, 10
Sellnow, T., 45

Shea, P., 17, 19, 21, 22, 23, 24, 42, 82, 83
Shea, T., 59
Sherer, P., 59
Sheridan, K., 46, 47, 81
Sherrill, J., 49
Shi, M., 45, 70
Shin, N., 50, 70, 71
Shin, S., 35
Shmerling, S., 28, 76
Shoup, R., 61, 68
Siemens, G., 48
Simpson, M., 70
Sindelar, T., 57
Singleton, E. S., 49, 79
Slagle, P., 47, 70
Smith, B. L., 32
Smith, S. U., 24
Song, L., 49, 79
Stefanou, C. R., 51
Stein, D. S., 47, 70
Stevens, M., 39, 59
Sullivan, F. R., 57
Sun, J. C., 50, 69
Sutton, S. C., 7
Swan, K. P., 17, 19, 21, 22, 23, 71, 84

T

Tandberg, D., 3
Taplin, M., 77
Taylor, C., 83
Terenzini, P. T., 7, 68, 75
Thompson, T. L., 31
Tinto, V., 5, 23, 32, 95
Tobias, S., 25
Trinko, L. A., 47, 70
Turner, J. C., 51

U

Umbach, P. D., 44, 46
Uzuner, S., 21, 42, 82

V

Valanides, N., 82
Vaughan, N. D., 22, 23, 71, 84
Vesper, N., 68
Vickers, J., 21, 24, 42, 82

W

Waldner, L., 45
Wankel, C., 60
Wanstreet, C. E., 47, 70
Watts, A., 48
Watts, M., 81
Wawrzynski, M. R., 44, 46
Wegerif, R., 32, 38
West, R. E., 21
Widener, M., 45
Williams, J., 28
Williams, J. P., 58, 59
Williamson-Whitney, V. A., 77
Wilson, G., 80

Wolverton, M., 33
Wu, Y., 44, 70

X

Xu, Y., 46

Y

Yalcin, S., 20

Z

Zach, L., 31
Zeng, H., 83
Zhao, C., 32
Zhu, Y., 42, 43, 44, 54, 57, 70, 80, 81, 82, 83

Subject Index

About the Author

Katrina A. Meyer is a professor of higher education at the University of Memphis and is an experienced researcher, totaling over 60 peer-reviewed research articles on online learning and technology in higher education published in national peer-reviewed journals. She is also the author of three earlier Association for the Study of Higher Education (ASHE) monographs: *Faculty Workload Studies* (1998), *Quality in Distance Education* (2002), and *Cost-Efficiencies in Online Learning* (2006). In 2009, she edited a *New Directions in Higher Education* volume, *Lessons Learned from Virtual Universities*. She is also on the editorial boards for three journals that publish research on online learning and technology in higher education (*Innovative Higher Education, The Internet and Higher Education,* and *Journal of Asynchronous Learning Networks,* now entitled *Online Learning*) and regularly presents her research at conferences hosted by the Online Learning Consortium. Prior to becoming a faculty person in 2001, she served for three years as the distance education director for the Nevada System of Higher Education and associate director for academic policy and planning for the Washington State Higher Education Coordinating Board for eight years. She earned her PhD from the University of Washington in 1984.

About the ASHE Higher Education Report Series

Since 1983, the ASHE (formerly ASHE-ERIC) Higher Education Report Series has been providing researchers, scholars, and practitioners with timely and substantive information on the critical issues facing higher education. Each monograph presents a definitive analysis of a higher education problem or issue, based on a thorough synthesis of significant literature and institutional experiences. Topics range from planning to diversity and multiculturalism, to performance indicators, to curricular innovations. The mission of the Series is to link the best of higher education research and practice to inform decision making and policy. The reports connect conventional wisdom with research and are designed to help busy individuals keep up with the higher education literature. Authors are scholars and practitioners in the academic community. Each report includes an executive summary, review of the pertinent literature, descriptions of effective educational practices, and a summary of key issues to keep in mind to improve educational policies and practice.

The Series is one of the most peer reviewed in higher education. A National Advisory Board made up of ASHE members reviews proposals. A National Review Board of ASHE scholars and practitioners reviews completed manuscripts. Six monographs are published each year, and they are approximately 144 pages in length. The reports are widely disseminated through Jossey-Bass and John Wiley & Sons, and they are available online to subscribing institutions through Wiley Online Library (http://wileyonlinelibrary.com).

Call for Proposals

The ASHE Higher Education Report Series is actively looking for proposals. We encourage you to contact one of the editors, Dr. Kelly Ward (kaward@wsu.edu) or Dr. Lisa Wolf-Wendel (lwolf@ku.edu), with your ideas.